LYDIA MILJAN AND BARRY COOPER

HIDDEN AGENDAS

How Journalists Influence the News

UBCPress · Vancouver · Toronto

09 08 07 06 05 04 03   5 4 3 2 1

Printed in Canada on acid-free paper

National Library of Canada Cataloguing in Publication Data

Miljan, Lydia A. (Lydia Anita), 1963-
     Hidden agendas : how journalists influence the news / Lydia Miljan and Barry Cooper.

     Includes bibliographical references and index.
     ISBN 0-7748-1019-X (bound); ISBN 07748-1020-3 (pbk)

     1. Journalism – Canada. 2. Mass media – Canada. I. Cooper, Barry, 1943- I. Title.
PN4908.M535 2003   071'.1   C2003-911088-5

Canadä

UBC Press gratefully acknowledges the financial support for our publishing program of the Government of Canada through the Book Publishing Industry Development Program (BPIDP), and of the Canada Council for the Arts, and the British Columbia Arts Council.

Printed and bound in Canada by Friesens
Set in Bembo and Venetian by Artegraphica Design Co. Ltd.
Proofreader: Judy Phillips
Indexer: Noeline Bridge

UBC Press
The University of British Columbia
2029 West Mall
Vancouver, BC V6T 1Z2
604-822-5959 / Fax: 604-822-6083
E-mail: info@ubcpress.ca
www.ubcpress.ca

FOR DEREK AND DENISE

"Let us now tackle the problem of journalism – deadliest of the weeds on Crabbe's Heath."

– CYRIL CONNOLLY

"Precisely because those in the media are persons of slight education, they depend on the intellectuals whom they surpass in beauty and income."

– HARVEY MANSFIELD JR.

"[The media] seem to be nothing in themselves, and often say that they merely report what goes on. In truth, they *do* nothing on their own; they act in the manner of a compassionate passerby who sees an accident in the street and rushes to see if someone else can be of any assistance. But the media greatly affect how we regard government."

– HARVEY MANSFIELD JR.

CONTENTS

FIGURES

PREFACE

The origin of this book is reflected in its dual authorship. In 1994, co-author Barry Cooper wrote an analysis of CBC television news, *Sins of Omission*. Among other things, that book examined news transcripts and compared what made it to air with other sources of information. The technique used is generally referred to as qualitative content analysis, and the conclusion, suggested by the title, was not just that a great deal of relevant information was omitted, but that it was deliberately omitted. As a result, TV news on CBC was both partial and systematically unbalanced.

As we indicate in the present book, there is considerable controversy about *why* the media present readers and audiences with the coverage they do. Much of this discourse is speculative, and ranges from the effects of time zones on how stories from California or British Columbia get treated in New York and Toronto to the attractiveness of journalism to thin-skinned people with narcissistic personalities.

One of the more obvious and perhaps important intervening variables between the raw reality of an event experienced in the world and the sophisticated and technically mediated product consumed through the flickering screen or the daily paper is the journalists – the actual reporters, producers, and editors who convert events into news. Some, but not all, of their choices are conditioned by the imperatives of deadlines, the requirements of the medium, or various other widespread and well-studied considerations. But some choices are also conditioned by the political opinions that journalists hold. Or so most commonsensical individuals might plausibly believe.

For media analysts, however, there is a problem – not so much to determine the extent to which the personal views of journalists influence the product, but to document the existence of an influence. The reason why this problem exists may be summarized by the claim that the news merely is a mirror to events because journalists simply report what happens.

The second source of this book, Lydia Miljan's doctoral dissertation, "The Backgrounds, Beliefs, and Reporting Practices of Canadian Journalists" (2000), is a sustained examination of the validity of journalists' conventional claim that, since they are "professionals," their views – whatever these may be – have no impact on the product, the news itself. In the course of this work, Miljan conducted a survey of the attitudes of Canadian journalists and compared these data to data simultaneously collected from the general population. Much of the evidence brought to light by that survey, the first ever so conducted in Canada, is reported in this book.

Together, these two studies constitute what the French call the *problématique* of the present book. Common sense indicates it's simply prudent to have an attitude of skepticism toward the notion that the beliefs of journalists have no effect on their reporting. The reason is simple enough: it is true that journalists have long claimed to be professionals, rather like doctors and lawyers and men and women of the cloth. But one difference is obvious: whatever your anesthesiologist may think about global warming, the fate of the swift fox, or the fiscal policy of the government of Prince Edward Island, that opinion is not likely to have a noticeable impact on her ability to administer an epidural. In contrast, reporting, producing, editing, or visualizing a story can never begin to approach the technical procedures of an anesthesiologist. Stories are told from perspectives: that is not an accident or defect, but the essence of stories. This book tells the story of where Canadian journalists tell their stories from.

Both sources for this book relied on the material collected in Canada's National Media Archive, of which Miljan has been the director since its inception in 1987. The archive is a division of the Fraser Institute and we would be gravely remiss if we did not first thank Dr. Michael Walker, executive director of the institute, for his intellectual support and a bracing managerial style that is such a refreshing change from that at most Canadian

universities. We would also like to express our gratitude to the Donner Canadian Foundation and the Earhart Foundation for their assistance in supporting the original study by Miljan.

Any undertaking of this magnitude depends on the good humour and
hard work not only of the authors but also, and more important, of the
people who aided in collecting the data. For the survey research we are
grateful for the advice, hard work, and good judgment of Conrad Winn and
his polling firm, COMPAS. It was Conrad who helped us shave costs and
encouraged us to include the general population portion of the public opinion survey. As for the content analysis, it could not have been done without
the hard work of four indefatigable research assistants who devoted their
summer months to reading, analyzing, and coding French and English news
content. We have had numerous research teams in the past, but this group far
outpaced our usual excellent talent. Avril Allen, Jonathan McFarlane, Timo-
thy Buckland, and Sue Hall went beyond the call of duty. We would also like
to thank our editors, Emily Andrew and Camilla Jenkins, for their support
and attention to detail.

As with all scientific work, whether in social, medical, or natural fields,
this study is incomplete. Accordingly we would like to thank, by anticipa-
tion, any readers who might find fault with our methods or disagree with
our interpretation. Critics are always to be welcomed, never to be feared. We
need to be informed of our errors as much as we would like to inform
others of our version of things. Besides, with two authors, the other one
made the mistake, so no one needs to feel embarrassed.

PART I

CONTEXT

CHAPTER I

WHY JOURNALISTS?

We begin with an example that has gained legendary notoriety among supporters of the Reform Party/Canadian Alliance. In April 1997, Canadian political parties and the media were gearing up for a spring election campaign. That campaign would centre on issues nearly devoid of substantive policy content, focusing instead on symbolic issues such as which political party was truly "Canadian." Perhaps most astonishing, at least for its supporters, one party, Reform, was labelled by the others and by the leaders of those parties as racist. The NDP leader, Alexa McDonough, stated that the Reform Party's stance on Quebec would incite civil war (Canadian Press 1997). Name calling by political opponents is certainly not new in election campaigns, nor is it new for the media to report those allegations. What was unusual is that on 22 April 1997 – before the campaign had begun – the media, on their own initiative, declared that Reform was racist. Peter Mansbridge, the anchor for Canadian Broadcasting Corporation's (CBC's) flagship news program, *The National,*[1] started the domestic segment of the news by linking the Reform and Liberal parties:

Mansbridge: Well, with an election just around the corner, all parties want to avoid controversy. But today, both Reform and the Liberals seemed to slip on one of the most dangerous topics of all: race. We have two reports. First, Saša Petricic, on Reform's false step.

Saša Petricic: For British Columbia, the Sikh community has become a potent political force for the Reform Party; commenting on that has become a potent political liability. Once again, bringing charges of racism, when Reform can least afford them. At issue, an interview Reform's chief BC organizer George Rigaux made to the *Vancouver Sun,* accusing the local Sikh temple of conspiring to nominate Sikhs to represent Sikhs in every party in the riding of Surrey Central.

When he finished discussing the issue, Petricic took comments from interested parties.

Petricic: The charge brought a quick reaction from Sikhs, including Reform's own candidate in the riding – Gurmant Grewal.

Grewal: Mr. Rigaux's comments are unacceptable to the community, and unacceptable to me.

Herb Dhaliwal (BC Liberal MP): I'm not surprised by those comments. I think it just shows the true colours of many of their members and what the Reform Party stand for.

After the Reform Party and others commented on the situation, Petricic wrapped up the story with this conclusion:

Petricic: Over the past three years, Reform has tried to put to rest charges of racism in the party. It's even threatened to sue opponents who make the accusation; but time and again, Reform's protests have been overshadowed by comments that seem to confirm the worst. In this case, at the worst possible time. Saša Petricic, CBC News, Ottawa.

No one but Petricic called the Reform Party racist: not the Reform candidate in the riding, and not the incumbent Liberal member of Parliament. A common technique on television news shows is to "segue" or link one story with its successor. Here the bridge was provided by the term *race*; in the next item reporter Neil MacDonald reported on a Liberal candidate who had changed his position on Aboriginal peoples and gained the nomination. Mansbridge set the stage by saying, "As for the Liberals, one of their candidates said today, his views on race have changed. Just before the last election, Hector Clouthier made some stinging comments about Native people. Those comments were not widely reported at the time, but CBC News has received a videotape of them, from an unknown source. Neil MacDonald now, with the tale of the tape." MacDonald described the candidate and his riding. He then showed clips that indicated Clouthier's position on Aboriginal issues:

[Clip] *Hector Clouthier (Liberal candidate):* But before you start worrying about what's in somebody else's backyard, I suggest you should take a look at your own. Many, many reserves, and I say this respectfully, leave a lot to be desired when it comes to proper management and cleanliness.

MacDonald: On Native land claims ...

[Clip] *Clouthier:* If you don't pay the piper my friend, you don't call the tune. The Natives are net consumers of public wealth on a scale that would simply astonish anyone who has lived or worked near them.

MacDonald: And on Native environmental policies ...

[Clip] *Clouthier:* They are saying we're not interested in money, and they want to get back to the land, and yet many of them are trying to wring every dollar they can get from the government from subsidies.

MacDonald: Those views were expressed by Clouthier just before the last election; as a result, the Liberals refused to let him stand for the party in 1993. He vowed to get even, ran as an independent, and lost. The Liberals then retaliated by expelling him and banning him from running as a Liberal for five years. Now, though, Clouthier is back: the party has changed its mind; all is forgiven. [Visual clips]
MacDonald: And today, a contrite Clouthier retracted the remarks completely.

Clouthier: I think they were rather obtuse, ill-headed, and just plain stupid. If anyone from the Aboriginal community took offence to those remarks that I made on the night of February 10th, 1992, I truly am sorry, and I regret having said them. I guess, what else can I say?

MacDonald: But on a local talk show in Pembroke, months after he made the first remarks, Clouthier was sure of his convictions.

[Clip] *Clouthier:* I stand by everything I said that night. I will not retract any statements whatsoever.

MacDonald: The official party line is that Clouthier should not be punished forever for a few remarks he made, a few years ago. Neil MacDonald, CBC News, Ottawa.

No one denounced Clouthier as a racist. No one, including Mansbridge and MacDonald, confirmed or disputed Clouthier's allegations or the attitude that evidently warranted an apology. In the British Columbia story, Petricic indicated that even commenting on the undisputed fact that the Sikh community was an important presence in both the Reform and Liberal parties had become "a potent political liability." No one in the media indicated that, in most instances, a pervasive understanding of political correctness prevented such comments, nor did anyone indicate what the consequences of silence might be.

Perhaps more important, in the BC Reform story no one except the reporter called the party racist. Was this a case of an anti-Reform attitude? Does it betray a more general "left-leaning" perspective? Or does it show that journalists are quick to revive past dramatic instances of name-calling? In both stories an individual or party was trying to change its past image, and on the surface, at least, CBC seemed to indicate it liked reformed Liberals, but not Reform. In the event, the Liberals were able to avoid the label "racist," whereas it dogged the Reform Party throughout the subsequent campaign. However politically incorrect both sets of comments may have been made to seem, neither was obviously incorrect in a factual sense.

Journalists often say that their negative focus and their critical treatment of people, issues, and events is not limited to people on the right of the political spectrum. They say they are also critical of the left. Indeed, for most journalists, this is what fairness and balance mean. Here, for example, one might consider the initial media coverage, in the United States, in Canada, and around the world, a few months later when President Bill Clinton's affair with one-time White House intern Monica Lewinsky became public. The president's wife, Hillary Rodham Clinton, went on national television to defend her husband. Her comments were widely and fully reported in Canada, including on the CBC national news. On the 27 January 1998

National she charged, "The great story here, for anybody willing to find it and write about it and explain it, is this vast right-wing conspiracy that has been conspiring against my husband since the day he announced for president."

Could this be true? Were the media complicit in a vast right-wing conspiracy against the president of the United States? If so, was the opposition justified on ideological grounds? Perhaps President Clinton rubbed journalists the wrong way, though the evidence that had been broadcast of his engaging personality seemed strong enough. A ready-made explanation for this charge by Mrs. Clinton lay close at hand: ratings, and thus profits. Lee Bacchus in a *Calgary Herald* story published on 28 January 1998 drew attention to this issue:

> But can you blame the broadcast media? If the Clinton affair has the dank smell of misplaced passions, it also reeks of the sweet aroma of money.
>
> CNN's Larry King doubled its seasonal average of viewers last Wednesday night. Fox News quadrupled its average. And the new Geraldo – even without scheduling a live demonstration of sexual techniques as he might have in the old days – averaged 1.1 million homes tuned in, up from his average of about half a million.

Moreover, the ratings-and-profits explanation seemed to be confirmed by the millions of viewers who watched Barbara Walters's two-hour prime-time interview with Monica Lewinsky after the end of the Senate impeachment trial. A negative spin to the news has often been attributed to the profit motive. But which perspective is the correct one? How can it be true that, on the one hand, the media are left-leaning and out to get right-of-centre politicians for ideological reasons, and on the other hand capitalistic and out to get left-leaning politicians in order to make money? That is one of the questions addressed by this study. What moves the media? Are they driven by the profit motive, or do the personal backgrounds and idiosyncratic opinions of journalists make a difference in the type of news we receive?

Critics on the left and on the right have their own reasons to find fault with the media. The argument has also been made, however, that "everyone" hates the media in the sense that the media can be blamed for the ills of society, irrespective of the critic's ideological position. Scholars, pundits, and the public alike attack the media for problems ranging from low voter turnout to teenage pregnancy, from crime in the streets to low self-esteem among elementary school boys. Well-respected authors, commentators, and journalists themselves have made careers attacking and criticizing the media. We consider some aspects of this question in the following chapter. It seems to us unclear a priori whether institutional constraints or the opinions of journalists have a greater effect on the production of news, but we begin from the position that reporting practices matter and that the individual attitudes of reporters can influence their reporting.

What follows includes a consideration of the kinds of things that are systematically excluded from media reports and to that extent revisits arguments made in earlier studies (Cooper 1994; Miljan and Cooper 1999). In keeping with the view that sins of omission are significant, we shall give an account of what we do not discuss in this book before indicating what we do consider.

The purpose of this work is not primarily an examination of the accuracy of news reporting – although some discussion of this question inevitably arises in our analysis of economic issues – but an analysis of the individuals who produce and present the news. Numerous studies examine the constraints of the newsroom and journalistic notions of professionalism and how the job limits their time. Other studies examine organizational routines and pressures such as government and advertisers. This is not one of them. We do not offer an apology for news reporting, nor do we provide criticism of the day-to-day workings of newsrooms in Canada. Those questions concern important problems in organizational behaviour, but they are not the focus of this study. There may be many things that influence how the news is reported; we focus our attention on only one of them: the journalists themselves.

News journalists are not the only members of the media who influence public opinion. For example, it has been suggested that US talk-show host Oprah Winfrey is more influential in Canada than all Canadian newscasters combined. The fact that the US Cattle Producers Association chose to sue her for comments made about beef illustrates the degree to which it respects her ability to sway the public. In Canada, media personalities such as hockey commentator Don Cherry also evoke strong opinions. Cherry's critical remarks about the Bloc Québécois resulted in Bell Canada pulling its advertising spots from broadcasts of Quebec hockey games and in an investigation by the CBC ombudsman. Granted, then, that television personalities may have influence with their audiences, they too are not the subjects of this inquiry. The influence of Oprah Winfrey in particular or of American media in general are worthy subjects for another study. Nor is the influence of the likes of Don Cherry, which may well be great, of concern here. Rather, we are interested, in part, in the people that Cherry complains about: the Quebec news media. We will compare French and English journalists in terms of their backgrounds, attitudes, and beliefs, and see how those factors influence their reporting of the news. Accordingly, we also examine the content of news in Canada and compare the way news is reported with the self-descriptions of journalists.

Our own most fundamental assumption begins with the notion that almost by definition the media are in the middle. They mediate. But what are they in the middle of? What do they mediate between (or among)? And who are those in the midst of the media? Those are the questions this study also addresses. To answer these and other questions, this study looks to journalists' opinions and values. These attitudes are compiled using standard polling techniques. That is, we interview a random sample of English- and French-speaking journalists. We ask them questions about where they work, who they vote for, and what they think about public policy issues. In addition, we conduct a simultaneous survey of the general public, asking the same questions. This allows us to see not only what journalists in Canada think but also how their views compare with the public they serve. Because these surveys are based on random sampling, we do not know who the journalists are. What we are able to do is generalize our findings to Canadian journalists working at that time. To make the link between journalists' opinions and media content we then conduct content analyses of several daily newspaper and television outlets. The journalist opinions on the economy, social issues, and national unity are compared statistically with the sample newspapers.

On the surface, the media are nothing more than communication facilitators, a means of bringing people together. Once they facilitate people coming together, however, how can such people be unaware of themselves as having come together? But this is a rough-and-ready meaning of what democracy is. Small wonder, then, that in modern democracies the media are accorded a place of great importance. This is not, therefore, a trivial and merely "academic" study.

We think the media are important in Canada, as in other democracies, and in this book we examine one of the reasons why they are important. We start with the most obvious and commonsensical observation: the media matter because they communicate the news. It is important in modern democracies to know what is new, which is what gives force to the very modern aphorism that nothing is as stale as yesterday's news. Entertainment shares with the news the characteristic of having to be up to date. Entertainment is about the latest trends, about what we ought to find entertaining. This is why some students of the media, notably Neil Postman (1985), have made a good case that television can do nothing but entertain.

We will leave this issue aside in order to make the observation that journalists do not think of themselves as mere entertainers. They are more important than that, not least of all because of the aforementioned importance of the media in Canadian and other democracies. The media are important in non-democratic regimes as well, but for different reasons. Our concern is the media in Canada, and the aspect of the importance we examine in this book is whether the opinions of journalists influence the news they produce. We think the opinions of journalists are important because those opinions influence the news they produce. The burden of this book is to prove it.

No doubt critics will dismiss this book as being irrelevant. Many media scholars, especially in the United States, have moved beyond discussions of media bias, claiming that it is "pointless and repetitive" (Dennis 1997, 119). Others point out that even if there are fluctuations in news content, these fluctuations are not systematic. More important for them is that the "bias" can "almost always be explained by factors outside the ideological thinking of individual journalists" (Bennett 2003, 29). We disagree. It is our view that it is not just random variation that shows that some media coverage favours one side over the other. It is not merely press routines, availability of sources, and day-to-day events that determine the news. Journalists do influence news coverage and that coverage does move in a certain direction.

More broadly, we are concerned about the ability of the media to effect social change. Using a standard set of questions, we have taken a snapshot of journalists' beliefs and we compare them with those of the Canadian public. We then compare journalists' attitudes toward several public policy issues, along with a profile of how the mass media report on these questions. We look at both English- and French-speaking journalists in Canada; we examine similarities and differences, the gap between the public and journalists when they are considered not only as groups but also as individuals.

The media are important not just because they facilitate the communication of the news but (according to media watchers, at least) because of what makes up the news – because of its content. By itself, the news does not exist: it comes into being because it is produced by the media. To that extent, the media are agents in society as well as transmission belts. Media analysts have said that the media change opinions, form opinions, and mould moral and social behaviour. In particular, television has been implicated in creating an increasingly violent society, a more tolerant society, and a more permissive society. Media critics and parents have worried whether the media condition young people to be more violent, and television has been linked to the decline of social capital in civil society and the growth of passivity. Whether any particular claim can, in fact, be confirmed may be secondary to the nearly unanimous view that the mass media play a major role in the lives of most North Americans. They are an essential constituent of modern life, at least to the extent that modern life would be something quite different in the absence of the media. Any number of public opinion polls have indicated that the public rely on and, more important, trust the news media to provide information on public policy issues. From the days of the Kent Commission (Canada 1981) to yesterday's Gallup Poll (Mazzuca 2001), television in particular has been regarded as the most popular means by which Canadians acquire news and information. Comparable data from the United States indicate the same reliance of the general population, the "mass public," on TV. Likewise, commentators, scholars, and analysts are nearly unanimous in the view that the media have been an important and growing component in what has come to be called the information age – the very term evokes the influence of the media. One thing seems certain: the media are in the middle of the political process. They claim to provide information to the public and shape the way people think about the world. Even if the degree to which the media shape the political agenda is open to debate, politicians and policy makers *believe* the media have an influence on public opinion. That belief influences the political process.

Even so, not everyone who studies the media thinks that journalists matter very much. According to the perspective adopted by these analysts, what counts is who owns the media, not who writes the story or who produces

the six o'clock news. We think that the views of journalists matter indepen-
dently of who owns the media, so our first task is to show why.

CULTURAL CRITICS VERSUS LIBERAL PLURALISTS

Generally speaking, scholars use two models to examine the media. One,
which we follow more or less faithfully in this book, holds that the power
and the importance of the media lie in the media's ability to influence the
formation and content of citizens' opinions. We may call this a liberal and pluralist perspective, because it assumes that public policy to some degree is the
outcome of a more or less reasonable and multi-part conversation among
citizens and political institutions to which they accord legitimacy.

The second approach, which well may command the allegiance of some
university-based analysts, uses a model that places the media in a position of
explicit social control: if you are concerned with the influence of the media,
this approach says, find out who owns what. We will call this the cultural
critical approach on the grounds that most of the practitioners describe
themselves as being engaged in "critical theory," or "cultural criticism," or
some other variety of discourse analysis or semiotics that can trace an intellectual pedigree back, eventually, to the work of Karl Marx.

One could also designate these cultural critics as Marxist, provided one
bears in mind that we are dealing not with a tightly disciplined doctrinal
sect so much as a common strategy devoted to the unmasking of the linea-
ments of power. Within that general interpretive strategy a number of distinct approaches are provided. Characteristically, however, cultural critics direct
their attention to élite organizations, and therefore focus a significant amount
of their analysis on media owners. When they do examine journalists, their
focus is less on the individuals' ideological beliefs and more on how the
journalistic system affects the individuals' work. When ideology is examined,
the focus is on the journalistic routines and the ruling system (Shoemaker
and Reese 1991, 183-207).

On the other side, many liberal pluralists for the most part ignore who
holds power; they assume that journalists are responsible for the words they
write and for choosing the sources they interview for their stories. For pluralists, society is an array of competing ideas and groups. They think it is
certainly possible for there to be unanimity of opinion and even a dominant

opinion, but it is highly unlikely that one view or one individual will domi-
nate all the time. Moreover, liberal pluralists are of the view that the autonomy of the media from the state, from business, and from interest groups
is real, not formal or empty. Thus pluralists argue that the question of media
ownership is separate from managerial control of media content, and that
journalists are relatively independent with respect to how they write their
stories. This does not preclude the possibility that, if a journalist persistently
or even deliberately wrote or produced stories that owners found offensive,
he or she could be informed of the displeasure of the boss or even fired. It
does, however, take issue with the assumption of the cultural critics and
Marxists that journalists are either toadies of the bosses or out of work; it
says this is not self-evidently true, despite the undoubted occurrence of confirming instances.

More specifically, we disagree with one of the major governing assumptions of conventional Marxism: that capitalist society is characterized by
class domination and class struggle, so that the media are part of a larger and
more general system of social control. The apparent plurality of views in a
democracy, according to the Marxists, is a sham. The rhetoric of a plurality
of voices and, indeed, the model of a conversation for them simply masks
the fact that the media in capitalist countries serve the "corporate state."
That is what counts. The public accepts the domination of the corporate
state only because of the approval by the media, which are also owned by big
conglomerates. Moreover the trend, and also therefore the undesirability, has
been enhanced in recent years by "convergence" (Gerbner et al. 1996).

Convergence refers to the same media organizations holding control in
different media outlets. It includes cross-ownership, such as a newspaper
chain owning television stations. Increasingly it has also come to mean news
companies owning entertainment and Internet companies. In short, the media,
and much else, are nothing but "superstructure"; the reality, say the Marxists,
is exploitive capitalism. The role of the media in capitalist society is to induce and support antirevolutionary "false consciousness." Whatever one may
think of the insights provided by this approach and of the logic employed to
obtain them, it is a venerable tradition that extends back to the writings of
Marx himself (Marx 1843).

In part, the Marxist approach and the cultural critical school derived from
it were an understandable reaction to what James Curran (1990, 137) called

the "American domination" of the media studies field, "with what seemed
to many of us at the time as its sterile consensus, its endless flow of repetitive
and inconclusive 'effects' studies situated in a largely 'taken-for-granted' pluralist model of society, and instead to generate a debate that reflected the
diversity of European intellectual thought."

The diversity of European thought that Curran and several others had in
mind was strongly influenced by the orthodox Marxist notion of false consciousness as well as the initially more heterodox, though increasingly re-
spectable, doctrine of "hegemony" developed by Italian Marxist Antonio
Gramsci. A hegemonic class, according to him, is the source of an order
diffused throughout civil society in such a way that it informs all taste, morality, and custom, and every ethical and religious principle – in short, all
social relations that have an intellectual or moral dimension. Marx's version
was simpler: "The ideas of the ruling class are in every epoch the ruling
ideas." It follows, Marx said, that "the class that has the means of material
production at its disposal has control at the same time over the means of
mental production, so that thereby, generally speaking, the ideas of those
who lack the means of mental production are subject to it" (Marx and Engels
1932, 172).

Likewise, Ralph Miliband (1969), a British Marxist, maintained that the
"engineering of consent" about which Gramsci wrote was the business of
private enterprise. By this argument, cultural institutions are a product of
civil or bourgeois society. The role of the media is to report on the dominant
institutions and figures of society. Marxist intellectuals have argued that the
media focus on official commentary, the words provided by presidents, prime
ministers, government, and business agencies, all of which invariably reinforce the hegemony of the capitalist system. They assume, for example,
that the stratification (and not the mobility) of North American society
means that the interests of the ruling class are bound to be in opposition to
the majority of the population, those who are ruled. Since Marxists assume
that politics is concerned with negotiating interests, they conclude that there
exists a "contradiction" between the interests of the rulers and the ruled that
must be explained.

Often the "contradiction" is described in an alarming way, as a danger to
democratic governance. For example, Robert McChesney, in the Preface to
Rich Media, Poor Democracy (1999, ix), declared there was a contradiction

"between a for-profit, highly concentrated, advertising-saturated, corporate media system and the communication requirements of a democratic society." McChesney was concerned with American ownership concentration, where the largest fifteen chains owned about a quarter of the newspapers; in Canada, 95 percent of the papers are owned by a half-dozen chains (Lorimer and Gasher 2001; Compaine 2000). For those who focus on ownership, then, the danger to Canadian democracy is even greater than in the United States.

Typically at this point in the argument, critical media theorists invoke the notion of hegemony to account for the ability of rulers to manage the contradiction. "The ruling class," wrote Robert Hackett (1991, 53), for example,

> needs to win allies and to maintain substantial popular consent with consent from below. On the one hand, the major agencies of ideological control (such as schools, churches, and the media) tend actively – though not necessarily deliberately – to disseminate dominant ways of understanding the world. So hegemony involves the permeation throughout most of North American society of a whole system of values, attitudes, beliefs, and morality that in one way or another supports the established order and the class interests that dominate it. On the other hand, ordinary people themselves accept the hegemonic ideology: It becomes enmeshed with the "common sense" through which people make their lives and their world intelligible.

The assumption guiding so many of the Marxist, Marx-inspired, or as the French say, *marxisant,* studies of the media is that the crucial factor is ownership. Ownership is the index by which power is indicated and deployed to manage the social and political contradictions of a capitalist society (Herman and Chomsky 1988, 592; Clement 1975, 287ff).

It is true enough that there has been a long-term trend in concentration of newspaper ownership in Canada (Kesterton 1967; Desbarats 1996). In late 1995 Hollinger Incorporated, led by Conrad Black, increased its Canadian newspaper holdings from a small chain of low-circulation papers to a chain that owned 56 percent of the newspapers in the country, accounting for 41 percent of newspaper circulation (Saunders et al. 1996). In response, many commentators voiced their deep anxieties about the consequences for democracy in Canada (Driedger 1996; Flavelle 1996; Barlow and Winter 1997).

An editorial in the left-wing *Canadian Dimension* was typical: "The effect [of the expansion of the newspaper holdings of Hollinger] is to viciously narrow the range of public debate, advancing corporate ideals while suffocating dissenting voices" (1996, 4). The remedy, at least for the anxious, was to pass laws regulating ownership concentration.

Similar proposals have been made in the past. In 1970, the Davey Committee proposed a press ownership review board (Canada 1970). In 1981, the Kent Commission proposed a Canadian newspaper act that would compel divestiture. As the commissioners said on the opening page of their report, "Freedom of the press is not a property right of owners. It is a right of the people. It is part of their right to free expression, inseparable from their right to inform themselves. The Commission believes that the key problem posed by its terms of reference is the limitation of those rights by undue concentration of ownership and control of the Canadian newspaper industry" (Canada 1981, 1). The recommendations of both the Davey Committee and the Kent Commission were never turned into law, largely because Canadians and their governments considered bureaucratic regulation to be a greater threat to a free press then concentration of ownership.

A study by Soderlund and Hildebrandt (2001) indicates that, despite the undoubted anxiety of critics, there is no evidence that the effects of Hollinger's acquisition impaired or threatened the existence of a free press in Canada. The study consisted of a "before and after" content analysis of a dozen papers, some of which were acquired by Hollinger, and some of which were not and so served as a control group. The question Soderlund and Hildebrandt examined was simple: did Hollinger, personified by Conrad Black, change the tone of his new papers to reflect his own opinions? They concluded,

> Contrary to the expectations advanced by critical theorists, our assessment (based on an analysis of their content over a six-year period) is that while changes in content and evaluation in these newspapers did take place, on balance, the thrust of the critical school hypotheses cannot be confirmed ... Our findings appear best described as *inconsistent* ... In some instances data confirmed critical expectations, in others they disconfirmed predicted trends, but in most instances they were simply inconclusive. Furthermore, in many instances, trends (both confirming and disconfirming hypothesized changes) were also evident in the various control papers, thus calling into question

whether ownership change was in fact the primary driving force behind the discovered change, suggesting instead that there were other factors, either industry-wide or specific to different regions or provinces, at work ... we found ... first, that while there were changes in content, not all that many of these changes were statistically significant. Second, for those changes that were statistically significant, not all moved in the same direction, nor could they reasonably be seen to follow discernable and consistent patterns. Finally, statistically significant changes tended to be found just about as often in papers which did not change owners as in those that did.

The reason why the anxieties of the cultural critics are misplaced is that newspapers are not just sources of information. They are businesses that must make profits for their owners and shareholders if they are to keep operating. Even the Kent Commission noticed this rather elementary reality (Hallman et al. 1981) and it has been confirmed many times (Demers 1996, 1999; Atkinson 1997). In the language of Soderlund and Hildebrandt, the kind of owner that would emerge after the Hollinger acquisitions – personified as "Conrad Black the committed ideologue or Conrad Black the shrewd businessman" – was never really in doubt.

Cultural critics, however, are not looking for mere empirical evidence of inconclusive effects. If the facts are not dramatic, they can be ignored (as the Curran quotation earlier in this chapter would have us believe) – or rather, they can be dismissed as being entirely unnecessary. As the Hackett quotation, also earlier in this chapter, indicates beyond doubt, an approach such as that followed by the cultural critics contains no requirement to show – by actually demonstrating their control of the content of communication – *how* media moguls exercise their alleged rule. It is enough to know that, by definition, they must exercise such control even when the evidence is nonexistent or inconclusive. Such an approach certainly simplifies media research. It also provides a ready-made model to account for all the other institutions of capitalist society. As with the operation of the media, there is no need to show how schools or churches operate to reinforce capitalism by careful empirical analysis of what they actually say or do.

It is our position that the notion of a necessary influence of media ownership on media content ought to be treated as a scientifically testable hypothesis rather than revealed and self-evident dogma. In fact, as we shall see, if ever in modern history the schools, the churches, and the media could plausibly be treated as elements of a unifying ruling structure, which is questionable, in modern society it is abundantly clear that they have grown further apart.

As an example of the failure of the critical school to engage in empirically testing their theories, communications scholar Thelma McCormack claimed in 1983 that the Canadian news media marginalized social movements: "But for those dissident social movements that are partially mobilized – feminists, environmentalists, peace movement people – the problem of access is different. On the one hand, it is non-recognition, and, on the other, it is a form of recognition that either discredits or trivializes the movements" (McCormack 1983, 469). These remarks were not based on any examination of the content of the news or on interviews with journalists. They were simply declared, *ex cathedra,* to be fact.

Even when cultural critics rely on quantitative data to support an assertion, they refer to non-empirical criticism to provide context. For example, sociologist Michael Clow found that from 1975 to 1983 the *Toronto Star* and the *Globe and Mail* marginalized the anti-nuclear movement. His conclusion was that *all* media treated the movement the same way, and that this was *typical* of how other social movements were treated by the press. At the start of his concluding chapter he stated that "Nuclear coverage is not an aberration from how social movements are generally treated" (Clow 1993, 91), and cited McCormack as an authority. Indeed, he elaborated McCormack's unsubstantiated opinion with the claim that "whether the subject is the environment, Free Trade, the Gulf War or women's issues, news coverage in the mainstream press seldom coherently reports the views of those who stand outside the 'common sense' of business and the political parties" (Clow 1993, 91). In fact, McCormack had provided no evidence to support the point Clow wished to make. Moreover, both her comments and the focus of his own study predate the North American Free Trade Agreement and the 1991 Gulf War.

Perhaps even more misleading is the effect of the highly abstract language favoured by practitioners of the cultural critical approach and by Marxists. In the Hackett quotation given earlier, the author argued that schools, churches, and the media tend "actively ... to disseminate dominant ways of understanding the world." The assumption seems to be that these social institutions somehow, and necessarily, provide ways of understanding the world so that no framework or conceptualization is needed to show how this alleged control is actually exercised. If institutions do the work, there is no need to acknowledge that people make up institutions.

As communications professor James Winter (1997, xvii) put it, "if individuals were factored into the analysis, then there would have to be some acknowledgement of individual differences." To acknowledge individual differences, however, would divert attention from the inexorable significance of institutions and "the system." Even worse, a focus on "individual differences" – which is to say, a focus on what actual journalists actually mean – would necessarily raise questions about the integrity of the hypothetical but also inevitable "huge monolithic system." Anyone working in the media who is not a willing participant in the huge monolithic system is, according to the argument of the cultural critics, necessarily marginalized as a "good journalist" engaged in an endless but also futile struggle.

Likewise there is no need for anyone such as Hackett to examine how schools, churches, and the media disseminate the "dominant" or ruling way of understanding the world. He provides no analysis of a single school curriculum. He is silent about the content of the dominant "ideology" of the churches, which are assumed to be homogeneous. Indeed, all organizations are treated as like minded. That North American society boasts different types of schools (secular, religious, private, public) and a variety of religious or spiritual leanings (Judaism, Buddhism, paganism, Christianity, Islam, Hinduism, "Eastern," and New Age, to name but a few), and that there are competing media organizations (private broadcasting, public broadcasting, chain newspapers, family newspapers, Internet publications, private publishers, and so forth) is majestically ignored.

The issue here is not one of empirical rigour, about which ferocious methodological controversies might swirl, but of an obliviousness to reality that ordinary common sense cannot ignore. Moreover, to common sense it seems tedious to have to point out that different organizations – the Catholic Church and most business organizations, for example – have very different positions, interests, and purposes. Contrast, for example, the mission statement of the Canadian Chamber of Commerce with that of the Canadian

Catholic Bishops. The main theme of the Catholic Church with respect to society is not one of capitalism and growth in prosperity and material wealth, but practically the opposite – social progress demands the government-directed redistribution of income. In contrast, the dominant ideology of most businesses is to make money for their owners or shareholders. How these contradictory positions illustrate a single ideology is not obvious. However strong the belief of Hackett and others of his persuasion (for Hackett is merely typical) that North American society can be reduced to a single interest and a single ideology, in the end the multiracial, multi-ethnic, and multidenominational social reality simply contradicts this opinion.

This is not to proclaim the dogmatic contrary, that there are no shared interests among journalists or that they have no common ideology. But it is not self-evident that politics is simply about interests, nor is it yet proven what the ideology of journalists might be or even whether their views are coherent enough to constitute an ideology in any meaningful sense. Even less has it been shown that this same reputed ideology is shared by media owners, other business people, religious leaders, educators, and so on.

Interestingly enough, when one reverses the logic of Marxist critical inquiry the results are no more satisfying. For example, Clement (1975, 125) argued that if one examined the way the Canadian "corporate élite" lived, it turned out that they gathered together in close-knit social circles: "They preside over the corporate world, using as their means of power, the central institutions of the Canadian economy – 113 dominant corporations, their subsidiaries, affiliates, investments, interlocking directorships with smaller corporations, family ties and shared class origins." So, of course, do the people who toil for the 113 dominant corporations gather in close-knit social circles with shared class origins. The language might be quaint – "113 dominant corporations" sounds a lot like Social Credit anxieties of the 1930s about the "50 big shots" – and the nature of Clement's information somewhat dated, but the logic could be applied today to formal and informal relationships among working people.

In 1996, for example, Statistics Canada's Labour Force Survey showed that roughly one-third of the Canadian workforce belongs to a union. That number increases significantly within certain occupations. Teachers and nurses are unionized to the 50 percent level. Three-quarters of public-sector employees belong to a union. Though only 26 percent of all journalists in Canada are union members, an additional 28.5 percent are covered by a union agreement (Akyeampong 1997, 45-54). The rate of unionization among journalists is underrepresented because the Labour Force Survey did not differentiate between self-described journalists and those in full-time employment. Full-time staff at the CBC, for example, and at most other television stations, are completely unionized. Similarly, newspaper staff are increasingly becoming part of the union membership. In Quebec, unionism is even stronger than in English-speaking Canada. Such statistical profiles are, naturally, interesting enough by themselves. But what, if anything, does it imply about the influence union membership has on the way journalists produce news?

According to the logic of the cultural critics and to the dialectical determinations of Marxism, journalists must either promote their union ideology in their work or suffer from "false consciousness." There are, of course, plenty of examples of where journalists use the rhetoric of their unions in their daily work. For example, in a CBC Newsworld (2 March 1999) interview with economist John Crispo on unionism in Canada, host Ben Chin quoted from his own union in questioning his guest: "To borrow a slogan from our own union, 'It's our turn.'" The unusual nature of union membership, as distinct from other social arrangements, is that unions overtly and deliberately try to influence their members on public policy issues. In this case at least, we have an example of a journalist using the information and rhetoric provided by his union to direct the questions to his interviewee. The real issue is, however, whether union membership leads to the widespread and systematic advocacy of union views.

Our data indicate that union membership alone no more provides an adequate account of the information presented in the news than do ownership patterns. Even so, the social relations of journalists, especially their union relations, have not been acknowledged in studies that focused on ownership. As a result, the effects of unionization on media organizations (if any) have gone unreported and so have been ignored.

Noam Chomsky, perhaps the best-known media analyst of the cultural critical school, has developed a complex propaganda model of the media. According to him, the way to understand the way news is produced and delivered is to examine the tried-and-true issue of ownership concentration; the reliance of the media on information provided by government, business, and experts who are funded and approved by these primary sources and agents of power; and what he calls "flak," which refers to the existence of groups that monitor and criticize the media (Herman and Chomsky 1988, 2). In his opinion, corporations fund flak groups in order to ensure that the media are forced to provide a market perspective.

In Canada, however, there are far more media-monitoring organizations that self-identify with the left than there are those who admire markets. One website devoted to helping journalists find story angles and sources on the Internet lists only the "flak" agencies on the left.[2] In introducing Julian Sher as the producer of JournalismNet, the CBC's Alison Smith said it was a website that many of those at CBC use (NewsMedia@CBC, 20 December 1998).

One obvious reason why the cultural critical school fails to resonate outside its own circles is that listing the holdings of media owners does not prove they control anything. The assumption that connects media ownership to media control has been cast into doubt by the anecdotal evidence provided even by adversarial journalists who question the existing pluralist social system and offer alternative solutions. Cultural critics have tried to brush aside such contrary evidence by dismissing it as indicating only "individual transgressions against dominant values (constitutional democracy, patriotism, national security, and so on) which are themselves taken for granted" (Hackett 1991, 83). But even individual transgressions contradict the dogma of a monistic ideology.

In any case, empirical studies show that values cannot be taken for granted by the media and that in fact members of the media are at the forefront of changing those values and ideals. Indeed, the evidence shows precisely that because values have shifted so dramatically over the past century they cannot possibly be taken for granted.

Statements alleging the media are a monolithic, undifferentiated group that "disseminate dominant ways of understanding" have been made without the benefit of information regarding what is actually being said and by whom. In order to determine what "ways of understanding" are in fact being disseminated, it is necessary to question individuals within media organizations who are in a position to make decisions about what counts as news.

It is all very well for cultural critics, critical theorists, and so on to draw links between the powerful and the media conglomerates, but it is also important to assess critically the views of people who actually make the day-to-day decisions. In the following chapter we address the even more basic question of why the news matters, and how the impact of the news on citizens in constitutional democracies has been examined.

CHAPTER 2

WHY THE NEWS?

Some members of society have always feared the mass media. The precursors to newspapers were often censored, limited, or otherwise regulated and controlled by the state. Newspapers in democratic nations were eventually granted freedom of expression, which in turn only served to heighten the fears of the influence of the press. The advent of radio, motion pictures, and television inspired new concerns about the effects of these new media because they provided the public with direct messages from advertisers, opinion leaders, and media personalities.

Early studies found that movies had both a direct and an indirect effect on the audience they served. One study (Blumer, reprint 1970), conducted from 1929 to 1932, involved a series of investigations designed to determine what effect motion pictures had on children. The fear was that when the broadcaster transmitted messages, those messages influenced the audience, which in turn caused great anxiety about the suggestibility of people, especially children. Blumer's views came to be known as the "magic bullet" theory or the "direct effects model." He found that children and young people would imitate the actors and actresses seen in the movies by copying their hairstyles and clothing. The chief limitation to his study was not so much that it discovered children "modelled" the images they saw on the silver screen, but that this "modelling" behaviour was generalized beyond imitation of glamorous movie stars into a general theory postulating that attitudes and behaviour on a wide range of other issues could be influenced and shaped.

Blumer used the diaries of his subjects as the basis for his argument, and it turned out that such sources were not a reliable basis for wider generalizations. It was not until more sophisticated experimental techniques were developed after the end of the Second World War that these broader issues could be addressed (McQuail 1979). However, the initial fear about the effects of new communications technologies never quite disappeared.

GENERAL MEDIA EFFECTS

The rise of totalitarian political movements and governments in Europe and the Soviet Union during the 1930s, as well as the continuing interest of scholars in the effects of advertising, increased anxieties in liberal democracies about the effects of the potential dangers of media exposure (see Hitler 1939, ch. 6). Studies sponsored by the Ohio Payne Fund during the 1920s and 1930s were motivated by an uneasiness about the fact that the media sent information directly to the public. The general concern for direct effects informed much of the subsequent research on wartime propaganda as well. Rather than confirming the direct effects proposed by previous researchers, however, wartime studies established that the media were *not* the powerful agents they were first believed to be and that, in fact, the media had a benign effect.

In part this new finding was a consequence of research techniques developed during the war in the fields of psychology and sociology. These techniques, innovative at the time, used surveys and scales to measure attitudes, and statistical analysis to measure the effects of messages on the public. In 1940 the limitations of research designs developed during previous decades were even more clearly exposed when US presidential election study researchers undertook face-to-face interviews with 1,000 Erie County, Ohio, voters. In the so-called Columbia studies, Paul Lazarsfeld and his associates argued that the media did not directly affect the public at all. Instead, there was a "two-step flow of communications" (Lazarsfeld et al. 1944; Berelson et al. 1954).

According to this new approach, "opinion leaders" received media messages and evaluated them; when the information conformed to their predispositions, these opinion leaders used it to influence others. The role of
interpersonal communication in disseminating and promoting ideas was
considered much more important than the explicit content of the media
messages themselves. American media researcher Joseph Klapper (1965), sum-
marizing the Columbia research, explained what now seems obvious: the
audience for mass communications comprised individuals who lived among
others in the midst of social institutions. These people already had attitudes
and opinions on a variety of topics and issues. Simply receiving new messages would not change their beliefs because in fact they preferred to read
magazines and newspapers or listen to radio programs that were in keeping
with what they already knew, felt, or believed.

The Columbia studies explained that the mass media were in the business
of reinforcing belief rather than introducing change, according to Klapper.
He suggested that selective exposure, on the part of audience members, and
the requirement, in a market society, that commercial media appeal to a
wide and varied audience (and thus would try to offend as few people as
possible) meant that the mass media would avoid controversial subjects and
so reinforce existing norms (Klapper 1965, 38).

The "two-step" theory and Klapper's subsequent elaboration of what it
meant theoretically may have allayed fears that radio (and then television)
had too great and too direct an influence on the political views of citizens,
but decades of research have nevertheless been devoted to showing that, in
fact, there are actual media effects. One explanation for this sustained research interest is that it is strongly counterintuitive to think the media have
no effect or merely small effects. In the context of twentieth-century history, which has surely been one of large-scale, rapid, and radical social change,
researchers have struggled with the question of why people's attitudes have
changed so frequently and over such short periods of time. It seemed obvious, perhaps even self-evident, that the rise of the new technological inno-
vations of radio and television had to have been part of the complex of
influences that have conditioned what we now call "value change." It is one
thing, however to "know" what "must be going on" and quite another to
give a reasoned account or explanation based on clear evidence.

One of these accounts (or theories) that has proven to be widely persuasive is usually called the "agenda-setting" theory. The argument is that, even
though the media might not have acted as a magic bullet or hypodermic
needle, they nevertheless set the public agenda and influenced what people
talked about by giving primacy to some issues over others. Unfortunately,
the data did not prove to be uniformly supportive. Until recently, researchers
argued that an agenda-setting effect was confined to unsophisticated audiences or undecided voters. Political scientist Robert Entman (1989), however, argued that by focusing on certain issues and not others, the media
indirectly told the public what to think by telling them what to think about.
The "way to control attitudes," he said, "is to provide a partial selection of
information for a person to think about, or process" (Entman 1989, 77; see
also Robinson and Sheehan 1982).

A significant proportion of quantitative empirical research has focused on
voters' attitudes during election campaigns. Often it deals with how the
media affects the impact of information on voters by comparing media
messages with information that they can gain from other sources. Thus, for
example, a negative media assessment of the US economy during the 1992
presidential election helped defeat George Bush, notwithstanding the evidence that, in fact, the economy had rebounded compared with a year or
two earlier (Hetherington 1996; Holbrook and Garland 1996).

It is more common and more conventional, however, to examine how
campaign information affects voters' evaluations of candidates. Conventional
research in this area assumes that the failure of the public to recollect basic
political facts, to recognize ideological leanings, or to recall candidate characteristics or names was a sign of an uninformed citizenry, from which the
conclusion was drawn that citizens were minimally influenced by media
messages, or perhaps not at all (Apter 1958; Dalger 1996).

Political scientist Samuel Popkin (1994) disputes this assertion by arguing
that members of the public do reason about candidates, parties, and issues.
While the voter may not recall every policy detail, the seemingly trivial aspects
of electoral politics resonate with what he labelled "low-information rationality." Low-information rationality is the way to describe the public's intui-
tions and how people mesh detailed media information as well as political
campaign advertising with their own experiences. Even though television

and newspaper coverage of election campaigns may emphasize trivial components of the campaign, Popkin argued, they nevertheless influence the individual voter's decision.

A few Canadian examples from recent years illustrate Popkin's point. During the 1997 federal election campaign, Bloc Québécois leader Gilles Duceppe was frequently ridiculed by journalists covering his photo ops. In one case, a particularly unflattering picture of him wearing a plastic hat that looked like a shower cap was shown coast to coast after he had visited a local cheese factory. The *Toronto Star*'s Robert McKenzie (1997) used that event to summarize the Bloc Québécois election performance. The image was so powerful that it was used repeatedly and continued to undermine the credibility of Duceppe for several years thereafter. In one sense, news clips and pictures showing Gilles Duceppe wearing a plastic cap at a cheese factory may be seen as detracting from the real issues of the campaign. Even so, it is as close to dogma as one ever finds in political campaigns not to let the candidate be photographed in any kind of funny-looking hat. It happened to Michael Dukakis when he was photographed in a tanker's helmet during the presidential campaign against George Bush; a photograph of Jean Chrétien wearing a United Nations infantry helmet *on backward* has been shown time and again to convey a powerful and critical image of his government's defence policy. In all these instances, the ridiculous image signalled to the public that the leader was unable to make prudent decisions.

A positive example of low-level rationality successfully communicated by television took place less than a year after the Liberals' 1997 victory. The day before the first balanced Canadian budget in thirty years, Prime Minister Chrétien gave Finance Minister Paul Martin a bottle of black ink. This story was the lead item on both CBC and CTV on 23 February 1998. Moreover, the picture of Chrétien tossing the bottle to Martin was widely reprinted in newspapers across the country. Chrétien's photo opportunity provided little information on the upcoming budget except for the promise that it would be balanced. The black ink symbolized, in the sense of reducing, concentrating, and trivializing, that rudimentary information. But it also provided sufficient information to convey the image or the visualization that the Liberal Party had again become competent and adept managers of the nation's economic affairs.

A third and equally memorable example took place during the 2000 federal election when Stockwell Day stood by Niagara Falls and indicated that, like the water in the Niagara River, Canadians were heading south to the United States (when the river in fact flowed north). Day's failure to grasp the direction the Niagara River flows was not just a mistake about Canadian geography. It indicated to Ontario voters that he knew little about what it means to live in Ontario, which carried the implication that he did not care much about the province either. The actual direction that the Niagara River flows was probably a surprise to most Canadians living outside the region, since the general direction of Great Lakes drainage flows from west to east. Indeed, to many Canadians living west of the Ontario border, criticizing Day on such a matter may simply have suggested that the "Eastern" media were being unfair to Day, much as Bloquiste voters in Quebec may have detected an anti-separatist, indeed anti-Quebec attitude in the ridiculing of Duceppe. For Ontario voters, however, Day's mistake showed he was not one of them and that any Alliance appeal to that province would take much more care and preparation. The rationality communicated by Duceppe's picture and Day's confusion over geography may have been low level, but it was still rational, and it mattered a great deal.

TELEVISION NEWS EFFECTS

Even though there have been sharp disagreements over the strength and impact of the media in general on political affairs, most researchers seem convinced that television in particular has a significant influence on its audiences. One of the reasons for the privileged position accorded television is its accessibility. No special skills are required to operate television technology. Audience literacy or education is no barrier to entry. As the price of television sets has fallen, income has ceased to prevent people from watching. In addition, the simple fact that it makes politics accessible to every viewer means television cannot be ignored in a democracy.

Much of the literature on communication effects, especially on TV, has been influenced by social psychology. This research indicates that people use shortcuts to form opinions on complex public policy issues. Political communication scholars Shanto Iyengar and Donald Kinder (1987) in *News*

That Matters argue that what they call the "priming" of issues shapes public understanding of what issues are important and how to judge them. The term "priming" is used to describe the way a news item is emphasized at the expense of other issues or events. More recently, Thomas Nelson and Donald Kinder (1996) found that the "framing" of issues moulded public understanding of the causes of problems and of the merits of alternative solutions. The term *framing* describes the context in which an issue is placed and the image by which it is diffused. Let us consider their evidence.

In a series of experiments Nelson and Kinder found that the way that issues respecting American poverty policy, federal spending on AIDS, and affirmative action in employment were framed resulted in differences in the way respondents identified with the targeted groups of beneficiaries. When news stories were presented as blaming a victim who was easily identified with a minority group, tolerance of that group by the respondents went down. When stories were framed counter to the stereotype, tolerance of the minority group went up. Other research came to similar conclusions when the media's portrayal of "hate groups" was examined. In one experiment, for example, Nelson et al. (1997) found that when Ku Klux Klan activity was framed in a news story as involving freedom of speech, participants expressed more tolerance for the KKK than participants who viewed a story on the Klan from the frame of public order. This type of experimental evidence indicates that the media can, indeed, persuade audiences.

Political scientist Doris Graber (1984) showed that very often TV audiences forget the factual basis for the conclusions they retain about a candidate. "Media facts," she said, are converted "into politically significant feelings and attitudes" but the facts themselves are forgotten. Others (Lodge et al. 1995) have argued that campaign events do not matter very much at all and what counts is the *type* of information the public receives during a campaign; "horse-race" coverage particularly – who is ahead, who is falling behind, who is about to make a stretch run – could influence the campaign contributions candidates received for their electoral bid (Mutz 1995). All of these considerations also look like low-level rationality.

The assumption underlying most of the research dealing with media effects is that, by focusing attention on one thing rather than another, the media (and especially television) influence *what* audiences think about and also *how* they think about these issues. The assumption is reasonable enough insofar as so-called events do not appear with an attached index number indicating their importance. In short, media selection of some events as being more important than others directs public attention and, one could argue, public resources, away from some problems and toward others.

In the public policy arena, often social groups, business interests, and advocacy groups compete equally for government assistance, for media attention, and especially for television exposure. Organizations able to place their cause, concern, or plea on the television agenda are more likely to obtain the outcome they desire, because television attention is usually followed by newspaper, radio, and magazine play, and increasingly by Internet penetration as well. In other words, the importance of the media resides not just in the measurable and direct influence it has on the public but also on the influence politicians and groups believe it has.

Journalists are likewise convinced of the power of the media. For example, a survey of 126 journalists before the 1993 Canadian federal election campaign found that 81 percent "thought the media would have a very significant effect on the outcome of the election" (Frizzell et al. 1994, ch. 7). In the wake of the Charlottetown accord, according to Elly Alboim, former CBC Ottawa bureau chief, politicians "regarded journalists as the handmaidens of the political élite, and new approaches were thought necessary to involve average Canadians in coverage of the election" (ibid., 89). No doubt the Liberal Party was convinced of the power of the media when it provided journalists with lavish creature comforts during the 1993 campaign. CBC reporter Keith Boag went so far as to describe it in a story: "Courting the media has always been part of the game, but in this campaign the Liberals are taking the game to a higher level. Take their media bus: it has seduced reporters. They're in love with it. Not only is it roomy and comfortable, with televisions, and so on, but each reporter also has a workspace with a table, a lamp, and a telephone, and there's a fax machine in the back" (*Sunday Report,* 12 September 1993). It is clear, then, that politicians are sensitive to media coverage of issues and that they perceive the media as being able to influence public opinion, which means they believe that what the media say matters a great deal.

Sometimes the arguments in support of media influence become over-subtle. Sociologist Michael Schudson (1990), for example, was curious about the discrepancy between President Ronald Reagan's low national approval rating and his reputation in Washington as the "great communicator." Schudson argued that Reagan was effective because he convinced Washington élites, including journalists, that the public in general was influenced by his television performance. This argument rested on the notion of what Schudson called the "third-person effect." That is, individuals would not admit to being influenced by television, but they believed that others, more gullible than they, were so influenced. In this instance, journalists and members of Congress viewed Reagan's television appearances with some cynicism, but at the same time they believed that the public could not see through his performance. That is, despite his low approval rating, the media were impressed with Reagan's television skills, projected their impressions on the public, and eventually the public came to believe what the journalists said – namely that the president was indeed a great communicator.

With power, or at least the perception of power, goes responsibility. In this area the media are usually criticized for being irresponsible. Granted the assumption that the media can influence the outcome of elections, many critics have also argued that either deliberately or inadvertently the media have undermined traditional authority with respect to parents and children, citizens, and leaders. To the extent that the reporting practices of journalists in fact weaken the authority of political leaders, they also help damage civic trust and involvement (see Meyrowitz 1996 and Fiske 1992). Television's emphasis on the trivial and the ever-shortening sound bite contributes to this development, as does an emphasis on the game, not the issues (Patterson 1994). The result reinforces voters' views of politicians and reduces citizens' sense of involvement.

Many of these concerns have been examined in the field of media studies, in the context of American politics, though they undoubtedly apply to Canada as well. Matthew Mendelsohn (1996) noted, for example, that CBC coverage of the 1993 federal election campaign framed the election almost entirely in terms of strategies and tactics. As a result of this focus, "motivation always equalled strategy. Policy positions were treated as a mere campaign device to attract voters." From such a perspective, prudent analysis of public policy is excluded from the start.

To make matters worse, Canadian journalists have come to rely increasingly on journalists themselves for interpretations. Reporters' remarks comprised roughly 80 percent of the television statements made during the 1993 federal election campaign. The end point in this development was indicated by headlines in the 17 April 1995 issue of *Maclean's* magazine concerning the departures of Pamela Wallin from CBC and of Keith Morrison from CTV. The doings of these two celebrity journalists, it seems, had become *part* of the news, and they themselves were no longer mere reporters of it.

Critics and members of the broadcast media alike have emphasized a number of other features of television news to suggest its enhanced importance. The argument has often been made that television matters because it provides visual images as well as words. The issue is, unquestionably, complex (see Cooper 1994, ch. 1), but in our view it is not so much images as their accessibility that counts. Audiences may well believe what they see, but they also see what they are told. Thus when television stories are repeated in newspapers and magazines, and on radio, they become parts of a widespread common stock of knowledge that is bound to influence the behaviour of citizens.

Narrative counts. The number of visuals accompanying a TV report are relatively small in comparison to the number of pictures of people simply talking. From the anchor to the politician, from the person interviewed on the street to exclusive chats with prime ministers, labour leaders, and captains of industry, much of what television shows to the public is people talking, dull, undramatic footage that captures the essence of an event. Many studies of television news reveal that the competition for visuals means that there are fewer pictures than one would expect. While it is possible to deconstruct camera angles or the quality of pictures, and to attribute great significance to these recondite issues, most television news consists of talking heads.

An even more basic feature of television news is that it is *produced* (see Miljan and Cooper 1999). When dramatic pictures are available, they are contextualized in a newscast by a wide array of prewritten verbal cues. Pictures are used to emphasize a point made verbally, and not to provide independent information. For example, during the second week of the 1988 federal election campaign, *The National* ran its lead story on problems in the Liberal Party centring on allegations that important Liberals had written letters a few weeks before the campaign indicating the need to dump John Turner as the leader. The letters were the focus of the news report. During segments when these documents were discussed, a graphic of Liberal Party stationery was presented on the screen. It was not made clear whether the pictures shown on screen were those of authentic letters from disgruntled Liberal Party officials or merely props to support the words of the anchor, Peter Mansbridge. The image, however, was of seemingly authentic Liberal documents that supported Mansbridge's narration.

Later in the story, to emphasize once more the problems of the Liberal campaign, Mansbridge talked about the Liberals' own pollster who had said that the Conservatives were in the lead. Then, in dramatic fashion, Mansbridge stated, "The Tories were sweeping, and a halo hovered over Brian Mulroney, a halo too firm to be knocked off" (see *On Balance,* November 1988). The picture that accompanied the biblical allusion was of Brian Mulroney standing on the stage in the glow of a bright spotlight with supporters and the crowd cheering him on. During election campaigns, audiences are regularly inundated with candidates on stage basking in the support of their public. Rarely, however, do reporters identify this stock tableau with a "halo." The Mansbridge story appeared to be signalling the public that an angelic Mulroney had already won the election – four weeks before the electorate would go to the polls.

The necessity of combining arresting images and dramatic narrative extends beyond elections. For example, one might argue that the 1992 Los Angeles race riots, in the aftermath of the decision of the jury in the Rodney King case, resulted in part from the influence of the media interpretation of the Rodney King videotape. Before and during the trial, the media repeatedly broadcast graphic footage of a home video showing King being beaten by Los Angeles policemen. The entire tape was rarely shown. In the aftermath of the acquittal of the police officers and during the ensuing riots, members of the media were astonished: how could the camera have lied?

Rick Salutin's *Globe and Mail* column (8 May 1992) was typical: "The videotape of King's beating by four LA cops seemed like a powerful, unequivocal image – a self-evident case of unnecessary brutality for any viewer. Yet the jury decided otherwise. How come?" If all the video contained were images of obviously brutal behaviour by the police, then the decision of the jury was difficult to grasp. What the public did not see, but which provides an answer to Salutin's rhetorically powerful yet incomplete question, was the defence presentation of the same videotape. During the trial, defence counsel argued that King was resisting arrest, and in fact the video showed him struggling with police officers. Even though the public and the jury saw the same pictures, the jury was given an additional visual and verbal context. Unfortunately for the citizens of Los Angeles, who saw the rioting as a result of the verdict, the public was never prepared for a possible acquittal. In the Rodney King trial, the media were so certain of their interpretation of the video that they failed to present the other side of the story, and so contributed to civil disorder.

NEWS AND ENTERTAINMENT

At one time the distinctions between news and entertainment were fairly clear. During the 1980s and 1990s, however, North American television news often looked more like entertainment, and at times entertainment programs contained more reasoned debate than public affairs programming. In one sense it is self-evident that TV news must be entertaining because otherwise no one would tune in. More than the technical requirements of effective television production are involved, however. For example, during the 1992 US presidential campaign, Vice-President Dan Quayle gave a speech in which he criticized Murphy Brown, a television situation comedy character, for promoting single motherhood as a neutral lifestyle choice (Campbell 1992, 11). Much of the controversy and discussion ridiculed Quayle for treating Murphy Brown as a real person, and not a fictitious character. And yet the Murphy Brown character existed and the lifestyle choice of the character was debated, which made the *issue* real. The reality that was projected, however, was not the social consequences of the breakdown of the American family, which was the serious issue that Quayle sought to raise, but an amusing election event.

Of course, Dan Quayle and the media were both aware that Murphy Brown was fictional. The importance of the episode for our purposes is that it illustrates the extent to which the standards that govern conduct in real life and on television entertainment programming have been blurred. Furthermore, it shows how remarks directed at TV entertainment for a quite different and serious purpose can be ignored and still have serious consequences, namely the reduction of the credibility of the American vice president.

The discussion of public policy and political issues did not originate with the fracas over Murphy Brown. American television entertainment programs

have dealt with public policy debates since the 1970s (Lichter et al. 1991;
Comstock 1980). But during the same time frame that television dramas and
sitcoms have arguably become more cerebral, television news seems to have
become more trivial. Critics have used the pejorative term *infotainment* to
describe news coverage of crime and sexual misconduct, drawing attention
to the fact that the production of news shows is influenced as much by the
imperatives of entertainment as it is by the allegedly lofty norms of journalistic professionalism, public service, and political beliefs (Taras 1990). Neil
Postman and Steve Powers (1992) insisted that even coverage of the 1991
Gulf War was packaged more to entertain than to inform.

Even more striking than the packaging of news is the trend for traditional news shows and public affairs programs such as CBC's *The National
Magazine* periodically to change their format from in-depth interviews and
documentaries to quiz shows. CBC's *National Magazine,* and before it *Sunday Report,* has from time to time brought in entertainment personalities,
journalists, authors, and former politicians – not to debate current public
policy, but to square off with each other in a Canadian trivia game.[1]

Granted that entertainment may be as politically important as news programs or, what amounts to the same thing, granted that news programs look
like entertainment and are consumed that way, a number of additional and
unobtrusive consequences follow. As long ago as the work of communication and culture studies experts Walter Ong (1982) and Marshall McLuhan
(1964), the observation was made that television is consumed passively. It is
not a medium with which one can argue. It is consumed in "real time," so
that if you are watching TV you cannot attend to other things. These formal
aspects of TV consumption have led a number of analysts to conclude that
extended television viewing influences audiences to do less. By providing
dramatic visualizations of political life, television encourages people to re-
treat in ever-increasing numbers from the public realm into the private.

Communication professor Joshua Meyrowitz, for example, argued that
electronic media create new "social environments" that make it more difficult for citizens to take part actively in political life, which has the consequence of rendering politics increasingly the preserve of the very few
(Meyrowitz 1985). From a slightly different perspective, political scientist
Robert Putnam documented how the advent of television has coincided
with (and in his view contributed to) the decline of civil society. Rather

than arguing that TV changes the social environment, Putnam (2000) says that it contributes to increased numbers of people staying at home and so being unable to participate in common activities. A decrease in membership in social groups and in political participation cannot be explained by education, occupation, or family instability. Moreover, Putnam discovered that people who read newspapers are avid joiners of groups, whereas people who watch a lot of television are more likely to be loners. In his words, "Each hour spent viewing television is associated with less social trust and less group membership, while each hour reading a newspaper is associated with more." Researcher James Simon also found that people who watch television vote at lower rates than those who obtain their news and information from newspapers (Simon 1996; see also Fallows 1997).

None of these studies indicated that watching news programs rather than game shows or hockey made any difference in political or social participation. The consensus appears to be that time spent watching TV, rather than the content of what is watched, is what counts.

Many have argued that the most influential news and television personalities are not journalists but talk show hosts. In the United States and Canada, talk show host Oprah Winfrey has become so popular and influential that a single show critical of the cattle business was said to have devalued the entire industry by 10 percent. The popularity of talk show hosts has had other economic implications as well. When Oprah Winfrey launched her book club, for example, the impact on sales of books selected for the Oprah Book Club was profound. In short, Winfrey has had an enormous impact on the North American public and is a powerful force on North American consumers (not to mention consumers elsewhere) – consumers who watched television. These consumers may or may not have bought beef on her advice, but many of them undoubtedly purchased books she selected.

The strategic purpose of television has always been to bring audiences and advertisers together, and the content of news, information, and entertainment programs has always been a subordinate part of that strategy (Barnow 1978). The perfection of this purpose is the home shopping channel. There is no pretence of providing entertainment at the cost of advertisement, because advertisements have become the entertainment. So far as human activity is concerned, the most important aspect of home shopping by television is the fact that consumers no longer have to leave their living rooms in order to make the purchase. All that is needed to participate in the market is a phone and a credit card. For critics concerned with the decline of social capital, when TV consumers purchase gadgets from home the most important consideration is not the efficiencies of the market, but the fact that these same people are not becoming members of service organizations, or even sporting clubs, and they are not engaging with friends, relatives, or even their own children. Indeed, they are not even going to the store to shop.

The demographic profile of the people who watch a lot of television in the United States and Canada is significant in this respect. The typical US television viewer is black and watches 40 percent more television than the population as a whole (De Roche and De Roche 1991). Canadians on average watch more than 21 hours of television a week. The highest viewership is in New Brunswick, Quebec, Nova Scotia, and Newfoundland. New Brunswickers on average watch 24 hours of television a week compared with 19.4 hours in Alberta. Francophone Canadians, heavily concentrated in Quebec, watch the most television in the country (Statistics Canada 2002). Their viewing time exceeds the national weekly average by nearly four hours. Within Quebec, francophones watch more television than anglophones in all age and sex groups. In all provinces women watch more television than do men. Those who spend their time watching a lot of television take part in politics at significantly lower rates, including the participation that takes the least effort, voting. One conclusion seems clear: media personalities such as Oprah Winfrey exercise their influence over people who are but lightly engaged politically.

The decline of social capital may be more significant than the importance of the shopping channel may at first suggest. Consider the following comparison: in the ancient city the difference between public and private life was fundamental; in the modern one it has nearly ceased to exist. Of course, citizenship was restricted in antiquity, and women, slaves, and all others who acted in the private realm were excluded from the political life and thereby denied a full or "higher" life. In many respects, television has contributed to making the modern mass publics into what the ancients would have considered slaves.

Television audiences focus their attention on what is visualized on their screens and as a result turn away from political life. Indeed, their plight may be worse than the slaves or women of the ancient city because, unlike the disenfranchised in ancient times, modern television watchers are voluntary nonparticipants. These remarks do not suggest a class-based criticism of television because the trend does not apply exclusively to the poor or underclass, but is true across all socioeconomic groups.

We concede that a great deal of television programming is directed at the private sphere and, indeed, at the privatization of what once was public, and that the focus of this study is on news and information programs – shows that, at least in principle, are concerned with public events. Granted as well that television can influence people's political attitudes, it seems to have had far greater impact on reducing political participation. As a result, while it may be intellectually interesting to see how the entertainment media influence political opinions of audiences, the fact that audiences tend not to act on their opinions has made the medium they rely on less important when the focus is on the public policy implications.

Since entertainment television and the shopping channel have a different focus than news programs – and notwithstanding the influence of entertainment imperatives on the production of television news – it makes sense to appraise the two kinds of television (or the two kinds of entertainment) by different, and perhaps even opposed, criteria (Alexander 1981). Moreover, even taking into account the largely nonpolitical impact of entertainment television, television news journalists and their product are still important because, as we noted above, politicians take indirect media effects into account even when direct media effects are muted.

JOURNALISTS MATTER

In the discussion of the cultural critical approach to media analysis in the previous chapter, we noted that, by and large, cultural critics pay little attention to individual journalists either in terms of what they actually produce or in terms of what journalists see their own role to be. For cultural critics, as for Marxists, the "media system" is biased because it relies on profits in order to exist and as a consequence media self-criticism is impossible (Tuchman 1978).

The perspective adopted in this study, which we have called a liberal and pluralist one, assumes that *who* produces the news influences the news product. In 1998, for example, when Kelly Crichton was made the executive producer of CBC's *The National,* a *Maclean's* article profiled her background: "Crichton reached the pinnacle of Canadian television as the newly appointed executive producer of CBC's *The National.* That puts her in hands-on charge of the network's flagship nightly news and public affairs program. To do so, she stepped *down* the CBC's corporate ladder from her previous post as head of English-language television news" (Wilson-Smith 1998a). Not taking into account Crichton's background, beliefs, or ideological leanings, a cultural critical approach might simply assume that since élites run the show Crichton's new position merely confirms the hegemonic role of the media. Élites rule and they rule for the dissemination of dominant capitalist values. But the common sense of the *Maclean's* writer indicated that Crichton's background also mattered. This is what he found: "Crichton is known as an activist with firm ideas of what she wants – and the credibility to implement them. Notes anchor Peter Mansbridge: 'Take a look at her résumé – there isn't a better-qualified person to take over. She has worked as a reporter, assignment editor, run the CBC's London bureau, and produced the investigative program, *The Fifth Estate.*' In her personal life, Crichton has been married to Mel Watkins – a retired professor and long-time NDP activist – since 1971, and has 3 adult children" (Wilson-Smith 1998a). The Crichton story illustrates that an "activist" married to a prominent left-wing professor can attain a position of power within a taxpayer-funded media organization. The contingencies of Crichton's biography reinforce the significance of the questions we are asking: is Crichton an anomaly or part of a larger group? And do her "firm ideas of what she wants" influence her selection of what is to count as news?

Despite the insights brought to light by cultural critics relying on a Marxist perspective, so much of their underlying model is based on a rejection of the fundamental principles of modern democracy that it is not particularly illuminating when the concern is with describing real media effects in an actual working democracy such as Canada. A cultural critical approach rejects out of hand any notion of approximate objectivity and balance, disparages private ownership of media, and is fundamentally in the business of changing the political system. Because the underlying Marxist theory is based on a radical change of the entire political and information system, it is difficult to discuss empirically real – as opposed to imagined or theoretical – media effects on the individual.

Perhaps more to the point, much of the Marxist and cultural critical hostility to the liberal pluralistic perspective is unjustified. Marxists and liberal pluralists alike see the media as playing a "strategic role in reinforcing dominant social norms and values that legitimise the social system" (Curran et al. 1982, 14), but it does not follow that the media are capable *only* of reinforcing existing predispositions in the "hegemonic" culture. If cultural critics are correct in their view that the media can support only the existing social order and not reflect or even anticipate social changes as well, it becomes difficult indeed to account persuasively for dramatic social changes and for the evident role the media play in making these changes part of the self-understanding of contemporary Canadian society.

One way for cultural critics to interpret the evidence, as was indicated in Chapter 1, is to claim that these instances are exceptions to the ruling structure of social control. Another is to introduce "dialectical" (or oxymoronic) considerations: covering a protest or a demonstration, in this perspective, becomes a means to defang and repackage a genuine protest and serve it up for mass consumption (Gitlin 1980). This is the same kind of thinking that is at home with concepts such as "repressive tolerance."

On the other side of the political spectrum, critics have argued that, because of a left-wing bias, the media are largely to blame for the decline of political and cultural institutions. Whatever its intuitive appeal, this interpretation has neither been tested nor proven empirically. Studies of media bias have invariably begun and ended with the analysis of media content. Such an approach can certainly illustrate media imbalances, but it offers weak evidence for the intentions, let alone the motivations, of members of the media. *Imbalance* may well be innocent, in the sense that it may occur as a result of "normal" constraints on the production of news – that it be timely, exciting, entertaining, and so on. *Bias,* however, is the result of the explicitly political beliefs and sympathies of a journalist intervening in such a way that the meaning or the spin of a particular story is directly affected.

Journalists pride themselves on being fair, but the public and media critics are not always convinced. Postman and Powers, for example, have argued that journalists cannot claim simply to be "professionals" because, when attempting to use purely descriptive language, a journalist cannot avoid expressing an attitude about what he or she is saying (Postman and Powers 1992, 101). Observations of this nature cause great irritation to journalists who insist that their professionalism means they can provide balance in their reporting. While CBC officially maintains that balanced and objective reporting is its highest ideal, its own ombudsman has argued that such an ideal really has no place in modern journalism. Quoting the likes of Robert Hackett and Yuezhi Zhao (1998), the CBC ombudsman accepted the perspective of the critical school, namely that objectivity, even if it is the stated goal of news organizations, cannot be the guiding principle of journalists themselves. He went on to endorse the view that the journalist is the sole judge of what should be the social responsibility of the media, and therefore of what his or her own responsibility must be. Accordingly, the various codes of conduct for journalists are simply guides to help them focus on their own sense of social responsibility. Perhaps window dressing would be the more accurate metaphor.

If it is true that journalists are responsible for the content of the information presented in the electronic newscasts and in the newspapers of the country, then it is a matter of some importance to examine the kinds of stories they disseminate and the focus they have. The National Media Archive (NMA) has analyzed the content of media coverage of more than 80 different economic and political issues as they appeared in Canadian news over the past decade.[2] One of the consistent findings has been that, on major issues, media coverage is not balanced and that the imbalance tended to favour the same position. Similar to what Lichter and his associates (1986) found in their study of the US media, Canadian journalists have tended to support left-of-centre positions. The following is a brief overview of some examples of imbalance described by the NMA.

When the National Media Archive compared television coverage of the first twenty months of the Alberta Conservative government under Ralph Klein with television coverage of the first twenty months of Ontario's NDP government under Bob Rae, the media slant was obvious and pronounced. The spending cuts in Alberta were presented by CBC and CTV national news to be far more controversial than the ballooning deficit in Ontario. Coverage of Ontario's escalating government deficit was framed as a need to fight recession and therefore was acceptable; CBC-TV accordingly gave slightly more positive than negative assessments of this policy decision (54 percent positive). In contrast, assessments of Alberta's spending cuts were almost always critical. Ninety-two percent of CBC's and 88 percent of CTV's assessments of Alberta's spending cuts were unfavourable (Miljan and Burns 1995a, 8: 2).

The same theme was observed when the 1990 and 1995 Ontario election campaigns were compared. The NMA found that CBC favoured Bob Rae in 1990 but was critical of Conservative leader Mike Harris in 1995. Positive descriptions of Rae outweighed negative descriptions of him by a two-to-one ratio. In contrast, CBC provided nine times as many negative as positive descriptions of Harris. While Bob Rae was called, among other things, "experienced," "a golden boy," and "bright," favourable commentary on Mike Harris was limited to "constructive." Where Rae was criticized for being "inexperienced," "lacking an agenda," and "radical," Harris was called "inexperienced," "a nobody," "a faceless Tory backbencher," "shambling," "a turkey," "Chainsaw Mike," "a thug," "Neanderthal," "plain stupid," "an ideologue," "radical," "mean-spirited," "Newt Gingrich," and "a Ralph Klein" (Miljan and Burns 1995b, 8: 6). The associations surrounding both Speaker Gingrich and Premier Klein were, in the minds of journalists, highly negative, which indicates clearly enough the direction of journalists' perceptions.

Similarly, in the 1991 provincial election campaign in British Columbia, NMA researchers found that local television news reported New Democratic policies favourably. Almost three-quarters of BCTV and more than two-thirds of local CBC news assessments supported NDP policies rather than criticized them. In contrast, Social Credit policies received mostly negative attention. Both stations were twice as likely to provide negative than positive commentary about Social Credit policies, which were policies of fiscal conservatism (Miljan 1991, 4: 7).

Other studies conducted by the National Media Archive found journalists expressed decidedly firm opinions on the economic and social issues examined (free trade, health care, privatization, and labour issues). For example, CBC reporters provided twice as many critical as favourable comments on privatization of government-provided services. This also held for the opinion of reporters on free trade. *Globe and Mail* reporters presented eight critical comments out of every ten regarding privatization, while their opinions on free trade were slightly more critical than favourable. On health care issues, both CBC and *Globe and Mail* reporters' comments consistently favoured publicly funded and operated systems rather than user-pay or any other alternative. On labour issues, reporters' views were significantly more pro-labour than pro-management (Miljan 1989a, 2: 6). In fact, *Globe and Mail* reporters' opinions were almost exclusively in favour of labour's position. In coverage of the environment, reporters presented the simplistic view that corporate greed was the cause of an environmental crisis (Miljan 1989b, 2: 9), the existence of which was unquestionably accepted (cf. Lomborg 2001). George Bain, a journalist of long standing, has provided several additional examples where the media served the Canadian public badly by yielding to political bias, ingrained negativity, and intellectual laziness (Bain 1994).

Imbalance was not confined to domestic issues. In an earlier study, one of the authors of this book concluded after examining extensive CBC television coverage of three long-term foreign affairs stories:

> Journalists are adversarial, it is said, but they also select their adversaries. The CBC was not adversarial towards Mikhail Gorbachev, but was so towards Ronald Reagan ... they treat the parties to conflict in different ways, as the CBC did in their coverage of Ethiopia and Mozambique ...The Soviet Union, and especially its leader, Mr. Gorbachev, embodied and symbolised progress. The United States embodied and symbolised deviance. In Africa, Soviet client-states, or states influenced by ideological fantasies once professed in the USSR, were surrogates for progress; the South African state was the embodiment and symbol of deviance ... it seems clear that the visualizations provided by the CBC of the Soviet Union and of their friends in Africa did, indeed, serve Soviet interests (Cooper 1994, 220).

However persuasive these analyses may have been regarding media *imbalance* or media *products,* they do not deal with the question of media *bias.* As was observed in *Sins of Omission,* we cannot know the intent of journalists when they say or write the things they do. Nor can we do more than speculate on how the values and sympathies of journalists are expressed in news coverage when the only evidence we have is unbalanced coverage, and no evidence of what journalists actually believe or hold dear. In short, all content analysis does is quantify what in fact journalists have said. The only people who have probed the inner world of journalists were Robert and Linda Lichter and Stanley Rothman in their 1986 study of the US media élite. Their study combined Thematic Aptitude Tests (TATs) and survey research and concluded that "journalists are liberal cosmopolitan in their outlook. They are liberal and reformist, quite critical of American social institutions, and supportive of the 'new morality,' which emerged in the 1960s." Rothman and his associates then showed that the ideological views the journalists held, often unconsciously, were also present and expressed in their work. The Rothman study was a trail-breaking effort and highly suggestive for the present project.

None of this necessarily contradicts the arguments of Marxists that owners also exert control or influence over the content of news. But it does indicate that journalists themselves also control a significant part of their product. The concerns we have with the critical or Marxist approach regarding ownership is that proponents nearly always fail to support their theoretical constructs with evidence. Questions that could be verified have been ignored in favour of strong but empirically empty rhetoric. Links have been made between owners and their properties, but apart from conjecture, little has been proven regarding the accuracy of the claims of owner influence. Whatever the influence of news owners, direct or indirect, malign or benign, it cannot be found by examining corporate holdings. If owners have any effect on the news it must be measured by the effect they have on the people who produce the news.

The first chapter considered the question "Why journalists?" We contrasted liberal pluralist literature with the writings of cultural critics, which argue that the media are not agents of social change, but agents of social control. We criticized that approach because researchers have not linked their theoretical arguments with empirical observations. Evidence that cultural critics have provided is not systematic but anecdotal. The belief that owners control news content has simply not been tested. We also summarized the research on media effects, which shows the power of the media and how it has helped change social relations, power structures, opinion formation, and civic action.

Our view is that news content is dependent on those who have a direct hand in collecting, creating, and packaging it. We begin from the assumption that the values, attitudes, and beliefs of those individuals influence the ultimate product. That does not mean owners have never put pressure on journalists, but that in order to examine the effects of owners on news production, we need to ask the journalists themselves about issues of chill, influence, and control. We are about to present the results and analysis of a survey of journalists on just this question. The assumption is that the best way to discover whether or how journalists and owners influence the news is to survey journalists themselves and examine the content of their reports. These issues are discussed in detail. Before considering them, however, it is necessary to examine another controversial issue, the relationship of journalists to social change.

CHAPTER 3

AGENTS OF CONTROL OR AGENTS OF CHANGE?

THE EMBEDDED STATE

Cultural critics have oversimplified the role of journalists in liberal societies. They have oversimplified the nature of liberal societies as well. Typically they have said that journalists are agents for social control because they view journalists as lapdogs to government and to their bosses, the media moguls, but also because the journalists are said to enforce moral codes of conduct on the citizenry. Edward Herman and Noam Chomsky (1988), for example, argue (on old-fashioned Stalinist grounds) that the non-communist media in the United States are in fact anti-Communist. They also argue that, because of the profit motive of media owners, the non-communist media are necessarily pro-capitalist. Whatever the validity of this view with respect to the American media, which is certainly questionable, Canadian media do not seem to conform to the description.

Content analyses of Canadian news reporting indicate clearly that the Canadian media focus on the negative side of the news. In a five-year longitudinal study of television news, the National Media Archive (NMA) found, for example, that economic growth was ignored, that increased GDP was assessed negatively, and that economic coverage increased dramatically during periods of economic downturn (Morrison and Miljan 1992, 5: 4). On poverty issues the media adopted the positions characteristic of the left (Miljan 1994, 7: 9); they also blamed corporations for alleged environmental problems

(Miljan 1989b, 2: 9). This pattern of reporting is clearly at odds with the position that the media uphold the capitalist system. If anything, it shows that they support state intervention in the market in pursuit of collective regulation and redistribution, not a typically capitalist view of public policy.

In the examples just indicated, the NMA found that, almost without exception, the media advocated increased government spending and regulation as the solution to the ills of society. When the Canadian dollar lost value, journalists sought out experts who asked for greater intervention by the Bank of Canada. On poverty issues, journalists sympathetically and uncritically reported the calls of social activists for increased funding to the poor. On the state of the environment, which was invariably reported to be in crisis, the most frequent proposal was more government regulation, even though regulation so often increased environmental problems rather than mitigated them. This pattern of reporting, rather than conforming to the capitalist propaganda model of the cultural critics' school, points to advocacy of an expanded state.

Interestingly enough, advocates of the cultural critical approach point to some similar examples to show how the media are biased against them. James Winter (1997) recounts, "The news media were instrumental in bringing down Bob Rae's NDP government in Ontario in 1995. They played a significant role in the resignation of NDP premier Mike Harcourt in British Columbia, with a relentless media campaign over a tempest in a teapot." Even when the evidence was irrefutable that the media support left-of-centre positions, including, as indicated above, the highly supportive coverage of the British Columbia NDP and of Premier Rae, theorists of the cultural critical school are unshaken in their devotion to the imperative of hegemonic discourse. Occasionally the argument is softened so that North American journalists are said to favour "responsible capitalism" (Gans 1979, 46-8), though the meaning and relative weight of noun and adjective are far from clear.

In contrast, liberal pluralists argue that journalists are more likely to be agents for social change than agents for social control; this school links journalists' criticism of society and government to a decline in the effectiveness of the institutions in society that transmit civility and stability between generations – tradition, in the literal sense of what is "handed over" from the old to the young.

Both approaches assume uncritically that Canada and similar constitutional democracies are fundamentally capitalist and that the private sphere or "society" is the seedbed of interests that exist in some degree of tension with, and at arm's length from, the state. At this point, despite the generally liberal pluralist perspective that *Hidden Agendas* follows on the media, it should be noted that we find a more reasonable and more accurate assumption from which to begin this particular discussion is that Canadian society is not simply capitalist, and that corporations and businesses do not hold the preponderance of power. The relationship between the Canadian state and Canadian society, including the economy, has very much been one of mutual interdependence. Historically, the role of administrative officials has been central to the operation of the Canadian economy and to the regulation and normalization of Canadian society. The role of the media in this complex has been not so much to denigrate and criticize government per se as to promote a specific kind of change, often by means of mobilizing the administrative capacity of the state.

Over the past quarter-century or so, political scientists have refocused their attention on the independent role of the state, which means chiefly officials, civil servants, and bureaucrats; the state is now seen as a political actor that is strategically placed to pursue policies that may well diverge from the official policies pursued by the elected government or the articulate preferences of social groups. The discovery (or rediscovery) that the state is in the business of shaping its own political environment, even in a democracy, is usually associated with the work of neo-institutionalist Theda Skocpol (1985). The argument, very simply, is that any set of political demands may as easily result from prior state action as from the action of private individuals or elected politicians.

In Canada, political scientist Alan Cairns is the source of much of the same kind of thinking, though Leslie Pal (1993) has adopted and expanded several of Cairns's arguments. Initially Cairns argued that competition among the eleven Canadian governments had led to, and enhanced, social fragmentation (Cairns 1988, ch. 5). Following the 1982 constitutional changes he advanced a more complex, two-pronged argument. First, he said, both the Canadian federal state – by which he meant both orders of government and not simply the government of Canada, or "Ottawa" – and Canadian society had become "fragmented."

Perhaps more important for our purposes, however, Cairns and Pal have both argued that the state is "embedded" in society. Alternatively one could speak of a politicized (or "etatized," as Chodak [1983] called the phenomenon) society, or civil society.

Metaphors of fragmentation and embeddedness and expressions such as *etatization* are tied to the perception that specific state organizations develop official and unofficial ties to equally specific non-state interest groups. In other words, in recent decades in Canada the state and society have become increasingly interconnected, perhaps even fused in some respects as a consequence of deliberate policy choices by the national and provincial governments. At the same time, this tighter connection has fragmented the state and increased social cleavages. That is, the Canadian state – both orders of government – has grown more diffuse and uncoordinated at the same time as Canadian society has become increasingly pluralistic and characterized by multiple allegiances and identities. The growth of the federal state in Canada is not, therefore, simply a "natural" outgrowth of the development, for example, of the welfare state, but has considerably more complex causes.

The data to indicate, *grosso modo,* this relatively novel phenomenon are found in the changed balance in public and private-sector expenditures. In 1867, for instance, public expenditures were under 6 percent of GDP. In 1950 they were more than 25 percent and by the 1980s were approaching 50 percent. Moreover, the provinces have increased their share of public expenditures markedly in recent years – from 48 percent in 1950 to nearly 60 percent by the mid-1980s (Lermer 1984, 129ff). Almost a quarter of the workforce in Canada is employed in the public sector, which means that a large number of Canadians have a dual relationship to the state, both as citizens and as employees (Banting 1986).

This expansion has not, however, resulted in the growth of a monolithic administrative tyranny. Canadians have adapted to the expansion of government coercion, inducement, oversight, incentives, and obligations in a way that is designed to turn the growth of the state to their own advantage and to influence the policy agenda before it is crystallized as a firm policy decision. Thus the increased scope of state activities and the increased visibility of the state in selectively distributing goods and services transmits, less obtrusively, the message that status, income, recognition, and power are not simply the reward of efforts in the marketplace or in the public arena, but may also be the result of administrative creativity and effort directed at the manipulation of the state. For strategically placed individuals and groups with the skills and resources to use the administrative system – including the courts – the increased size, visibility, and importance of the state is an opportunity as much as a burden because such people can use it to their advantage.

The increasing ambiguity over where the state ends and society or the private sector begins is indicated by another novelty. The actions of individuals and interest groups do not necessarily precede legislation. Legislation is, therefore, not necessarily a *response* to interest group activity; on the contrary, state action – legislation – may *evoke* interest-group reaction either as opportunistic responses to a new legal, statutory, or indeed constitutional environment, or as integral parts of the legislation itself. As an example of the deliberate legislative creation of interest groups, consider the following: in 1969, cabinet authorized the secretary of state to create a Social Action Branch and charged this new office with the task of "social animation." As Pal observed, the notion of social animation amounted to "an in-depth attack on mass apathy" by recruiting, "sensitizing, and preparing" existing or potential social leaders (Pal 1993, 102-3). Moreover, social animation by government officials during the 1970s became a model for the implementation of what have become known as "postmaterialist" or "new social movement" visions during the 1980s and 1990s, an issue to which we return later in connection with the discussion of the attitudinal profile typical of journalists in Canada.

At the same time as the federal state has grown larger, the divisions between the national and the provincial governments have grown deeper. In 1945, for example, there were a total of 118 cabinet ministers in Canada. Forty years later, with the addition of one small province, there were 269 (Cairns 1995, 87). The significance of this increase is not merely that there has been a multiplication of cabinet portfolios and more faces around the cabinet table, but that each of those additional ministers presides over additional functionaries scattered across the provinces and the country in a bewildering and largely uncoordinated variety of departments, agencies, boards, commissions, Crown corporations, and other administrative units.

Some are scrutinized by ministers but others are free-standing administrative bodies – political orphans in the sense that they are relatively immune from legislative or sometimes even executive oversight. One implication is that any effort to challenge the decisions, or even the existence, of such administrative entities is necessarily directed toward the courts because there seems to be nowhere else to turn. Moreover, the fragmentation produced by this proliferation of government bodies has led to efforts at centralization and control, particularly by Ottawa, which in turn has created other strains and fragmentation (Savoie 1999).

To summarize the point being made: the embedded state is a relatively new phenomenon in Canada. It may well be true that "the more we relate to one another through the state, the more divided we seem to become" (Cairns 1995, 33), but that also means that the context for understanding the role of the media in Canada is one in which the several societies of this country are caught in webs of interdependence with the several states. This is why the assumption that both Marxists and pluralists make regarding the importance, indeed the centrality, of capitalism is, we believe, untenable.

If journalists, in fact, upheld a dominant or hegemonic ideology, then it would find expression within the embedded state, or at least with one of the "nodes" of state-society connection. We would expect, therefore, that journalists to the same degree as government officials or interest groups would be able to embrace the opinion that, at least on some issues, social ills can be solved by greater state intervention and control in people's lives. On the other hand, if Marxists were correct and Western society were in fact dominated by markets and capitalism, then we might expect to find supportive journalists helping business by exposing the dangers of bureaucracy and the undesirability of increasing the embeddedness of the state in Canada.

In fact, however, the connection between the state and the media is also one of mutual interdependence. One of the most obvious instances of this interdependence stems from the fact that state officials, by nature, turn out large volumes of material to meet the needs of news organizations for reliable, scheduled news flows. Mark Fishman (1980, 193) calls this "the principle of bureaucratic affinity: only other bureaucracies can satisfy the input needs of a news bureaucracy." The reason journalists go to government officials as information sources is straightforward and has many times been documented: because journalists report political events, they are a central part of both the political structure and the political process (Garnham 1986).

Journalists participate in the political process; like other participants, at one time they may promote the values, interests, ideas, and policy of government and at other times they may criticize them, but either way, they have a clear and an immediate interest to ensure that the political system or the regime keeps operating. In his discussion of the vested interests of federal politicians in keeping the national government strong, political columnist Gordon Gibson noted that "'Ottawa' is a set of specific interests that are paid for by all Canadians, but that really work for themselves. This same rule is personal and institutional survival" (Gibson 1994, 22). The first rule of personal and institutional survival applies to journalists as well as to politicians. In order to criticize "the system," the system has to continue to exist, so that criticism is often both a direct demand for change within the system and an indirect source of support for it.

For example, journalists are central to the maintenance of the symbolic component of government. Political scientist Francis Fukuyama recalled the argument that democracy needs people to uphold its normative beliefs: "Democratic societies cannot survive for long if people do not believe democracy to be a legitimate form of government" (Fukuyama 1995, 7). Likewise, Chomsky was certainly correct in his assertion that the media uphold the dominant liberal ideology of democracy. Few journalists openly support the suppression of free speech or advocate dictatorship since to do so would amount to vocational suicide. In regimes that do not allow free expression of political ideas or criticism of government, journalists play a diminished role, and often a dangerous one. The same requirement is not true with respect to markets and capitalism. Journalists need not promote capitalist interests to uphold the embedded state, even while criticizing it.

Likewise, neo-institutionalists James March and Johan Olsen (1989) have emphasized the importance of structures or institutions, whose operations are governed by what they called the rules of the game, namely "routines, procedures, conventions, roles, strategies, organizational forms and technologies around which political activity [or process] is constructed." Institutions are important, they argue, because they shape and at times determine human behaviour. As one of the many institutions of the modern state, the media have a role to play in upholding the entire configuration of institutions. For example, under this theory Ottawa-based journalists clearly have interests at stake in the matter of Quebec separation. In some areas of reporting they are bound to uphold the Canadian state. Therefore, even though they may be part of the problem in diminished public respect for institutions, the one institution that English-Canadian journalists might be expected to uphold is that of a nation united. At the same time, journalists in Quebec operate from a different perspective. Quebec-based journalists have fewer institutional ties to Ottawa, and therefore may be more likely to present and even support alternatives to their audiences. While the dominant embedded interest in Canada is to maintain the federal state, a significant interest in Quebec is devoted to creating a new state, and one might well anticipate journalists' support for it.

In fact, there is ample evidence that historically journalists in Quebec have promoted the desirability of the embedded state at least in that province. In his history of *La Presse,* for example, Pierre Godin found that during the Quiet Revolution the press and government both adhered to the same general position that state-directed "social progress" was a desirable public policy (see Sauvageau 1981, 44). Similarly, Dominique Clift argued in 1980 that, "identification with social progress was so great that a large proportion of the Parliamentary Press Gallery in Quebec City became almost an adjunct of the party in power" (Clift 1980, 214).

French-speaking journalists in Quebec have editorialized in their reporting of the news far more than their colleagues writing in the English-language press. Although the party press had largely been replaced by an independent one by 1936, Quebec journalists have strongly maintained over the years that their job is as much to form as to report opinions. Quoting Jean Hamelin and André Beaulieu's comment (1966) that journalists were more often "editorialists than reporters," influential *La Presse* journalist Lysiane Gagnon was moved to add that this was "perhaps a sign that the need to 'form' rather than 'inform' still dominated" (Gagnon 1981, 27). This attitude existed in the 1980s when Jean Paré, editor of *L'Actualité,* accused the French press of "chronicling the uses of power, whether in politics, unionism or finance ... [The press] seeks to influence rather than to reflect; there are too many people who *think* and not enough who have *seen*" (ibid., 28).

The direct ties between journalists and politics have also been strong in Quebec. René Lévesque and Claude Ryan, for example, were both well-known journalists before they went into politics. Even Jacques Parizeau and

Yves Michaud were managers of the short-lived Parti Québécois paper *Le Jour*. We might expect, therefore, that Quebec journalists, even if critical of the Quebec government, will still support the embedded Quebec state. Likewise, we expect that even if they show no support for the embedded national state, or what is called the federalist position in Quebec, that rejection does not so much entail a rejection of etatization as it does support for its more focused application and indifference to how politics is conducted beyond the borders of the province.

That the proper context for a study of the media in Canada is the embedded state receives additional support from the examination of Canadian news sources by sociology and criminology professor Richard Ericson and his team. The media mediates, they argued, by participation: "To the extent that contemporary politics is more a matter of symbolic representation than direct participation, it is arguable that journalistic participation in politics has never been greater. Journalists join with politicians and civil servants in giving direction to social order, and in doing so have an instrumental role in the political process" (Ericson et al. 1989, 173).

This description illustrates clearly how one institution, the media, faces both ways within the embedded state or the politicized civil society. Governments are of course necessary to establish the policy agenda; they may even be primary, at least in terms of symbolic representation. In one sense this observation is beyond dispute: governments have the advertising budgets and the public relations apparatus to determine what will become important and so to define the political agenda. Even so, Ericson et al. wrote, "reporters are literally part of the legislature and its political processes" (ibid., 252). They meant figuratively, not literally, but the point remains.

New roles and responsibilities for the state have also created what Marxists have called a new class, chiefly consisting of administrators and social activists whose fortunes have risen with the rise of the state, but including journalists as well. On occasion the privileges and benefits that go with important social status have caught the attention of other, less exalted, journalists. For example, when the CBC sent 50 employees to the Banff Television Festival in the spring of 1999, the story made the front page of the *National Post*. The story revealed that some CBC employees had booked a week's stay for the festival and were accommodated at the "elegant Banff Springs Hotel, where guests pay an average of $570 a night" (Galloway 1999,

A1). The story emphasized how privileged these people were by recalling as well that the corporation has often been described as "cash strapped." Such evidence does not bolster the credibility of Marxist analysis. As we noted earlier, when confronted with contrary empirical evidence, critical school theorists occasionally have argued that the ruling system was in fact not seamless and that North American capitalism "has adapted to the growth of monopoly and the expansion of the suffrage by allowing ideological space for state economic intervention and for social welfare measures" (Hackett 1991, 58). With so flexible a doctrine, it is hard to see how any evidence could disconfirm it.

Rather than seeing the media as agents for the dominant class or uttering a dogma that there is a liberal pluralist media, we intend to show that some ideas resonate more with media practitioners than do others.

The conclusion we would draw from these reflections on the context within which the media in Canada operate is that both the cultural critics and the liberal pluralists make arguments abstracted from the reality of common experience. We follow the methods of liberal pluralists more or less faithfully, but it does not mean that we must be uncritical of their theoretical underpinning on the matter of how journalists influence the news process. Because of the context of the embedded state in this country, we might expect journalists, as participants, to promote its goals actively, though not necessarily deliberately.

POSTMATERIALIST VALUES

Postmaterialist theory, which developed relatively recently, helps explain why some ideas, positions, and policies resonate more with the views of journalists than do others. Postmaterialist theory accounts for both the increased obsolescence of the left-right cleavage in politics and the rise of what are now called new social movements (NSMs). Its central assumption is that the better educated and wealthier a society becomes, the more public policy concerns move from economic subsistence and the role of the (pre-embedded) state in the economy to a concern with "higher order" issues, chiefly matters such as human rights, feminism, and environmentalism, all of which are understood as expressions of a voluntaristic "self." Postmaterialists tend to have better-than-average education and their demographic profile indicates they have lived nearly their entire lives in times of general peace and economic prosperity.

Postmaterialism is part of a general theory of new social movements. Sociologist Steven Buechler (1995) argues that NSM theories "emerged in large part as a response to the inadequacies of classical Marxism for analysing collective action." According to him, the two central pillars of classical Marxism – an economic explanation of politics, and class-based social and political analysis – were sufficiently misleading to make the doctrine incapable of offering a plausible account of contemporary forms of collective action. Marxist economic analysis presumed that politically significant social action sprang from the "economic logic of capitalistic production" and that in consequence all other social interactions were secondary. The focus on class conflict likewise presumed that social action be defined chiefly by class relations, which made all other interactions secondary. Because commonsensical observation of feminism, environmentalism, and the like indicated that they violated both basic assumptions of classical Marxist analysis, it was necessary to examine factors other than economics and class to account for the kind of collective action undertaken by NSMs.

The most obvious factors to be considered in any revision were that politics, ideology, and culture must be understood as fundamentally independent variables, not "superstructure" or a secondary symptom of more fundamental economic factors. A concern with NSMs, therefore, refers to more or less conventional social science research devoted to the configuration of collective actions that have evidently displaced the kind of activity that was to lead to the proletarian revolution Marxism expected and devout Marxists sought to help bring about.

Our concern is less with the genesis and typology of NSM theories than with the postmaterialist values that theorists such as Buechler introduce to account for contemporary political action: "In a society increasingly shaped by information and signs, social movements play an important role as messages that express oppositional tendencies and modalities. The very focus on personal, spiritual, or expressive aspects of modern life typical of new social movements is an implicit repudiation of the instrumental rationality of the dominant society" (ibid., 446). Other accounts have noted as well that the chief feature distinguishing NSMs from traditional political ideals associated with social order and prosperity – and so making them "new" – is their advocacy of anti-growth, libertarian, and populist social purposes. In addition, the political style of these movements often involves a conscious avoidance or a rejection of institutionalized politics undertaken within established political parties.

The most comprehensive account of the shift from an emphasis on material well-being and physical security to one focusing on quality-of-life issues is provided in a series of books by Ron Inglehart (1977, 1990, 1995, 1997; and 1996 [Inglehart et al.]). Canadian political scientist Neil Nevitte (1996) has applied many of Inglehart's insights to Canada. These studies show that individuals who tend to support "materialist" values such as maintaining order or fighting inflation are in many other ways distinct from individuals who give more emphasis to "postmaterialist" values centred on self-expression. Moreover, this value shift has resulted in a highly focused and often single-issue public becoming involved in politics and taking on an active role in research, agenda-setting, advocacy, and policy development.[1] Inglehart argues that this change in values expresses a "decline in the legitimacy of hierarchical authority, patriotism, religion and so on, which leads to declining confidence in institutions" (Inglehart 1977, 4). According to him, the mass media are one of the *sources* of this change in values, rather than a means of reflecting the change to a wider public.

Although Inglehart does not go into detail on how the process of value change is assisted by the media, he does make the general observation that the media often transmit information that threatens existing societies. "The mass media," he said, "are a force for change, since they communicate dissatisfaction, alternative lifestyles, and dissonant signals, even when they are directly controlled by the 'Establishment'" (ibid., 11). Inglehart identifies two distinct kinds of media influence: first, the media increase the knowledge and sophistication of the public; second, they also convey opposition to existing or conventional values and traditions. Inglehart does not, however, indicate whether members of the media themselves have been at the forefront of the value change he documents.

A postmaterialist account of the ideological predispositions of NSMs and of the role of the media within this social and political complex is not the same as a postmodern one. Insofar as the media are concerned, a postmodernist would claim that audiences cannot be manipulated or duped by the media. Audiences, according to postmodernists, make (or make up) their own meanings using the media and whatever else may be at hand or in the mind to construct "a cultural politics of resistance." The motivation of such a cultural politics obviously must come from elsewhere. We are not making any postmodernist claims: following Inglehart's line, we argue that the media should be closely examined because they have significant influence on the audiences they serve.

Paul Abramson and Inglehart (1987) projected that by the year 2000 about 17 percent of the western European population would be postmaterialist. Other evidence suggests that the cohort of postmaterialist journalists may be larger. For example, Peter Drier (1982) noted that after the 1960s journalists were more likely to be have received post-secondary education, chiefly in the social sciences and law, than before. Moreover, North American journalism schools emphasized "interpretative reporting, analysis and background" (Drier 1982, 120). Rather than having been trained to be a mirror that reflects the affairs of the world to readers – however imperfectly they carry out their task; whatever flaws, cracks, and bumps the mirror may have – the younger journalists are more likely to have been trained to be what sociologist John Johnstone and his colleagues (1976) called "participatory journalists," that is, people who perceive their role as shaping and even creating news. Those working for major newspapers and magazines are valued for providing background, context, and interpretation. They usually sympathized with the social movements of the 1960s and 1970s, with the result, according to Johnstone, that news critical of government and business institutions increased. In short, contemporary journalists appear to share both in the demographics and in the attitudes typical of Inglehart's postmaterialists.

Accordingly, we expect journalists to be more postmaterialist than the Canadian population as a whole so that, rather than reflecting the dominance of the class system, as Marxist or Marx-derived cultural critical perspectives would lead us to expect, they would be more likely to champion postmaterialist causes in the stories they report.[2] Consequently, we expect the dominant ideology found in the media will not be one of promoting the capitalist system nor of a frontal attack on it, but of promoting a particular kind of postmaterialist social change.

When journalists promote social change, however, they necessarily reject the guidelines of objectivity – and, again, it is a separate question to consider the extent to which any particular act of reporting is fair, balanced, accurate, or objective (in *any* sense of these terms). To promote social change, which means always to promote a specific social change, is to advocate, and advocates do not usually *try* to be fair, balanced, objective, and so on. Typically journalists justify their advocacy on the grounds that they believe they are right, and that what they advocate will improve society. Such a self-understanding, as Robert Lichter and his colleagues observed, is also typical of unreflective and narcissistic personalities (Lichter et al. 1986).

Anecdotal accounts suggest that Canadian journalists are likely to share this trait with their American colleagues. In a review of Jan Wong's *Globe and Mail* column, for example, *National Post* columnist John Fraser (1999) made these comments: "I also think she is probably like most high-risk journalists I know: insecure, surprisingly resentful of criticism despite all the stuff they dish out, desperate for appreciation, both proud and guilty of the special vantage point they have on current affairs and powerful people, and somewhat naïve about the power they wield." In short, Wong and other "high-risk journalists" display typical attributes of narcissists.

The point about narcissism as a personality trait or personality type is not that journalists are psychologically disordered or pathological human beings. Even less are we making a moral judgment. Rather, as with such terms as "inner-directed" and "other-directed," a narcissist can live a life well within the bounds of ordinariness, including moral ordinariness, and still be distinct as a type. To speak of someone as narcissistic is not the same as saying someone is obsessively narcissistic or compulsively so. Rather, as the Lichter team quite properly said, there are two sides to narcissism. One is an "adequate basis of positive self-feeling, which enables the individual to weather life's ups and downs." The dark side associated with narcissism includes selfishness and egotism. Narcissistic behaviour results in enhancing one's self-esteem by projecting one's undesirable qualities onto others. "In general, the narcissistic person uses others primarily to regulate his or her own self-esteems, rather than treating them as separate individuals with their own needs and identities" (Lichter et al. 1986, 103-4).

When the Lichter team measured the narcissism of journalists as compared to business people, the former outscored the latter consistently, at statistically significant levels, on both measures used. The implication that may reasonably be drawn from studies such as the one done by the Lichter team is that a good dose of narcissism in one's personality helps make one an aggressive journalist and it indicates a personality trait that might justify presenting and promoting a personal world view.

In addition to anecdotes retailed, for example, by one journalist (Fraser) about another (Wong), occasionally journalists confess their own motives and elaborate upon the perspectives they have adopted. René Lévesque, for example, told the following story about his own days as a radio reporter, covering the first trip behind the Iron Curtain by Lester Pearson, in 1955 still minister of external affairs. During the visit Lévesque recorded an exchange between Nikita Khrushchev (then first secretary of the Communist Party of the USSR) and Pearson. Khrushchev apparently had attacked Pearson for representing an "American colony." Lévesque's story made the front pages in papers in Brussels, Paris, and London. However, when he came back to Montreal he discovered that Pearson did not care for the story and had had it embargoed. Lévesque was told that he could release the story after the embargo had been lifted. His reaction and commentary about the incident reveal much about his future aspirations: "Thanks a lot. There's nothing deader than old news. I blew my top, blasted them as they deserved for political censorship, and came out of there feeling like jumping over a cliff and with a solid and enduring antipathy for that cautious collection of Canadian mandarins. Under my fellow journalists' by-lines I'd been able to read my story everywhere, but here at home the most colourful scoop of my career had been suppressed to protect the dignity of Lester Pearson. It was enough to make one ... separatist!" (Lévesque 1986, 136).

While one would expect journalists to be upset about the suppression of their news stories, only someone with a highly ambivalent sense of his own importance and self-worth would turn a professional problem with state bureaucrats and, to be sure, a narcissistic minister of the Crown into a personal affront that promised to have dire political consequences down the road.

Previous studies of journalists have tended to avoid the entire issue of value orientation and instead focused on journalists' own perceptions of their role in society or in the newsroom, or else they focus on journalists' attitudes toward owners. Often they cite Jeremy Tunstall's examination of journalism as an occupation focused on the goals, roles, and demands on the individual (1971). Similarly Lee Becker and his associates (1987) focused their research on how US journalists were trained and their prospects for employment. Canadian surveys of journalists likewise have sought to describe what journalists thought about their role and responsibilities, with little probing into their attitudes and predispositions. For example, Hawley Black's comparative study of French and English journalists was devoid of any questions on voting behaviour, ideological leanings, or attitudes on public policy issues (Black 1967). Instead it examined the role of journalists in general, their role in English–French relations, and their opinion of their industry.

Communication scholar Gertrude Robinson's survey of women newspaper journalists examined 106 Canadian dailies to "determine the number, distribution, organization position, average salary and professional beat covered by both male and female journalists across the country" (Robinson 1981, 2). Similarly Lysiane Gagnon's study of journalism and ideology in Quebec asked questions about the factors and functions of journalists' work, but had no specific queries about journalists' attitudes on major issues of the day or about their political leanings (Gagnon 1981). Indeed, in the Royal Commission on Newspapers directed by Tom Kent there was no attempt to examine the journalists' attitudes on anything outside their own industry.

That is not to say that no one has examined the values of journalists, but that such studies have not been done in Canada. There have been studies of the attitudes of Australian (Hennigham 1998), British (Delano and Hennigham 1995), and American (Lichter et al. 1986) journalists. Even though this work has not achieved the prominence of the cultural critical approach, it has provided a number of useful insights with respect to foreign journalists that might profitably be explored in a Canadian context.

DESIGN OF THIS STUDY

The primary research focus of this study is on the political orientation of journalists. We therefore focus upon what journalists believe about politics and how they report political issues. In order to make comparisons between journalists and Canadians in general, in 1997 we empanelled a representative sample of Canadians and another of journalists. We interviewed a general population sample of 804 Canadians along with 270 journalists, working through a professional survey research institute, COMPAS, in Ottawa.

COMPAS interviewed respondents over the telephone in either English or French.

The general population sample of Canadians was a straightforward stratified random sample. Determining the composition of the journalist sample was more complicated. The principle that defined the journalist population sample was that members worked in the major news organizations in the country. We wanted a mix of newspapers, television, and radio, as well as a mix of private and public organizations. We also sought to have a mix of management and "front-line" journalists – reporters, editorial writers, and columnists.

In addition to comparing journalists as a group with the general population, we sought to determine whether there were any significant differences among groups of journalists. Postmaterialist theory holds, for example, that with greater education and urbanization comes a greater propensity for postmaterialist values. Accordingly, we structured the study to compare opinions of journalists on these and several other dimensions.

This study is unique. It is the first analysis to compare the way Canadian journalists respond to questions on the economy, social issues, and national unity with how these stories were reported in Canadian news outlets. By comparing journalists' attitudes with their reporting practices, we can better detect the linkages between ideology and reporting. The chief problem with previous content analysis studies was that this type of linkage was rarely provided. In a content analysis of the past twenty-five years of *Journalism Quarterly,* for example, communication scholars Daniel Riffe and Alan Freitag (1997, 522) found that while there was an increase in the use of studies employing content analysis, that growth was not "paired with increased theoretical grounding, nor with more frequent formulation of explicit research questions or hypotheses." This study has both a theoretical component that links the content of media production to the ideological position of journalists, and an explicit complex of research questions and hypotheses, centred on postmaterialism. In other words, we examine the extent to which Inglehart's assumption of journalists being at the forefront of social change is correct. If it is, we should find journalists expressing postmaterialist values in greater numbers than the general population.

PART 2

DATA

CHAPTER 4

WHO STAFF CANADA'S MEDIA?

During the winter of 1997 and 1998 we conducted half-hour telephone interviews with 123 English-speaking journalists employed by Canada's most influential media outlets: the *Globe and Mail*, the *Toronto Star*, the *Financial Post*, selected Southam and Sun chain newspapers, as well as the news organizations of CBC (radio and television), CTV, and Baton Broadcasting. The same questionnaire was administered to 55 French-speaking journalists at analogous francophone media outlets: *Le Devoir*, *Le Soleil*, *Le Journal de Québec*, as well as the television and radio services of Radio-Canada. Within each organization, individuals were selected randomly from senior news staffs. In the print media, reporters, columnists, bureau chiefs, and editors were sampled. In television and radio, we selected correspondents, anchors, and producers. The result is a systematic sample of the men and women who put together the news at Canada's most important media outlets.

Also included in the sample were 147 English-speaking journalists who worked primarily in small-market radio, TV, and newspapers. They show significantly different attitudes from those of English-speaking journalists in larger markets working for major urban papers. We have excluded them from this analysis because they are less likely to be opinion leaders or agenda setters than their higher profile colleagues, who are our present concern. Small-market media often take Canadian Press (CP) stories, or stories from the chains (e.g., Southam/CanWest), and reproduce them with very little change. The Penticton or Prince Albert papers will rerun a story from the big-city papers, not vice versa. That is why the big-market papers are agenda setters, and the small-market papers follow them. We found there were no statistically significant differences between small- and large-market French-speaking journalists and so included them all in the analysis.

This study explicitly does not interview Canadian Press journalists. The reason is that one of our objectives was to compare major dailies owned by different chains and to indicate the limitations of the "cultural critics" perspective, which ascribes great importance to ownership, but since CP is not "owned" the way the *Vancouver Sun* or the *Globe and Mail* are owned, we saw no reason to survey CP staffers.

We also conducted a general population survey of 626 English-speaking Canadians and 178 French-speaking Canadians to obtain data so as to compare the views of the general Canadian population with the media sample and to determine how their attitudes and beliefs are similar or different from that of the media population.[1] We begin with an analysis of the data from the English-speaking sample and follow it with an analysis of French speakers. The questions asked are reproduced in Appendix A.

ENGLISH-SPEAKING MEDIA PERSONNEL

Demographics

In very few respects are English-speaking journalists typical of the audience they serve. In general, these journalists are well educated, non-religious men in their forties. In contrast, the English-speaking general population sample consists of nearly equal numbers of men and women who do not hold university degrees, with median ages in their twenties and thirties. For those not familiar with measures of central tendency, the median simply refers to the midpoint in the data distribution: it is where 50 percent of the cases fall above and 50 percent below.

It has become the norm for journalists in Canada to hold post-secondary degrees: 59 percent of English-speaking Canadian journalists are university graduates; a further 14 percent hold post-graduate degrees. In contrast, 45 percent of the English-speaking general population has high school education or less. Twenty-two percent of the general population has a university degree.

English-speaking journalists are more likely to be married or living common-law than the general population. Sixty-seven percent of the journalist population is married, compared with 55 percent of the general population. Journalists also have a higher rate of living with a partner than do the general population (8 percent compared with 4 percent). In addition, fewer journalists reported that they have never been married compared with the general population (14 percent compared with 25 percent, respectively of the journalist and general populations).

Although English-language journalists typically do not have children living at home, they do not have significantly different reproductive rates than the general population. Half of the general population sample indicates no children living at home, compared with 41 percent of the journalist sample. The median number of children for journalists is one, whereas the median for the general population is zero. The mean number of children for the general population is 0.96 compared with 1.19 for journalists.[2] There are no statistically significant differences between the two groups in the number of children living at home.

Journalists are most likely to be in their thirties and forties. Thirty-two percent of English-speaking journalists are in their thirties and 43 percent are in their forties. In contrast, figures for the general population are spread more evenly: 24 percent are under thirty; 27 percent are in their thirties; 16 percent are in their forties.

Journalists are also less likely to belong to a religious denomination than the general public. Sixty-one percent of the English-speaking general population indicate that they belong to a religious denomination, compared with 42 percent of journalists. As with the American media élite, members of the Canadian media are also more secular than the general public in their outlook.

On the issue of faith, 32 percent of English-speaking Canadian journalists said that they definitely believe in God compared with 66 percent of the general population. Only 5 percent of the general population said they definitely did not believe in God, compared with 14 percent of the journalists. In other words, journalists are nearly three times as likely not to believe in God than the general public. Consequently, members of the journalist population are not regular churchgoers. More than three-quarters of journalists attend religious services fifteen or fewer times in the year. Fifteen percent make an effort to attend services on a regular basis. The average attendance is nine times a year; the median is less than once a year. Although the question regarding church attendance was inadvertently left out of the general population survey, we know from other research that the journalist attendance is lower than the already low general population attendance: 23 percent of Canadians attend church regularly (Bibby 1993, 6). However, English-speaking Canadian journalists are 10 percent less likely never to attend services than are their American counterparts; 76 percent of the Canadian journalists never or seldom go to services, compared with 86 percent of the American media élite (Lichter et al. 1986, 22).

What is somewhat unusual in our sample of journalists is the relatively high number who declare their religion to be Roman Catholic and yet do not attend church regularly. Sixty-two percent of those in the English-speaking sample who declared themselves as Catholic do not attend mass on a regular basis. This is higher than the general population. According to sociologist Reginald Bibby, 49 percent of Catholics in English-speaking Canada attended church two or more times a month compared with 38 percent of the Catholic journalists (1987, 20). Over the past few decades, however, attendance in all religious denominations has been on the decline (Bibby 1993, 7-8). Journalists who indicate they are Roman Catholics attend less regularly than other Catholics. Thus, even if Canadian journalists are disproportionately Catholic, they are still more secular than are other Canadians, which is consistent with the hypothesis that they are at the forefront of postmaterialist social change. The assumption is that if they are postmaterialistic in their value orientations, those values will be presented in the news they report. This in turn can explain why society has changed in general, with journalists acting as the vanguard.

Probably the single largest difference between the general population and that of journalists is the under-representation of women in the higher echelons of the profession. Despite gender parity in the general population, journalism – at least in the higher levels – is still largely male dominated. Seventy-seven percent of the English-speaking journalists surveyed were male.

Traditional images of journalists evoke the romanticism of a hard-living and hard-drinking lifestyle. As Christie Blatchford, then of the *National Post*, indicated in an interview on CBC's *Undercurrents* (1 November 1998), "The old-time days, I think, of journalism, like the old-time days of a lot of businesses, are subtly gone, where – and I was never really a part of that – where hard-drinking, hard-living kind of romantic world, I mean it's a business." Notwithstanding the decline of the hard-drinking days, there are some indications that members of the journalist community drink alcoholic beverages more than the general population. When the question is, "Approximately how many days in a typical week would you have a beer or other alcoholic beverage?" the median number for English-speaking journalists is two, the median for the general population is one. The mean number of days per week in response to this question is 2.33 for journalists compared with a mean of 1.54 for the general population. The difference, although small, was statistically significant at the 99 percent level. In other words, even if the numbers do not indicate that the hard-drinking lifestyle typically associated with journalism still exists, the data do show that journalists are less likely *not* to drink than are the general population.

One might argue that the differences just indicated might better reflect the fact that journalists are an élite group, because the same results would be expected to emerge for any élite group compared with the general population. However, when we compared similarly educated Canadians from our general population survey, we found that the élite journalists also have few similarities with them. For example, university-educated Canadians believe in God more than do journalists, are less likely to be married, and are younger than the journalist sample. Most telling are the differences in education and gender between the various groups. In the general English-speaking population, 42 percent of the sample are female and hold a university degree. In contrast, 23 percent of the journalists are female. Figure 4.1 summarizes the main findings of the demographic information comparing the English-speaking university-educated public (i.e., a subgroup of the broader group used for the figures above) and journalist samples. Marital status and the number of children might be explained by journalists being simply representative of an élite group, but the other demographic elements seem to be more indicative of the journalists themselves.

On the basis of these basic and preliminary data, one thing can be stated with confidence: the demographic profile of journalists is more consistent with postmaterialist demographics than is the profile of the Canadian population as a whole or than other university-educated Canadians. We now turn

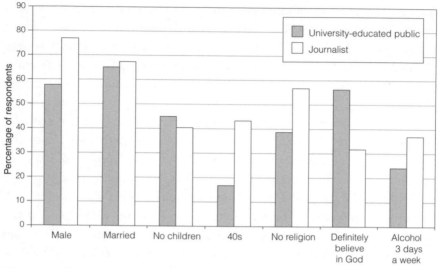

Figure 4.1   Social background of English-speaking educated public and journalist
samples, December 1997-January 1998

to questions of ideology to see to what extent journalists are similar to, or
different from, the general population.

Ideology

Demographics can tell only one part of the story. Simply because an individual exhibits certain characteristics, it does not follow that he or she will
exhibit specific beliefs or behaviour. Here we consider whether journalists
have values that differ from the general population and plot their location
on a conventional left-right political spectrum.

   A number of studies that have examined journalists' values do so by comparing voting behaviour and the self-positioning of respondents on an ideological scale. For example, surveys in the United States have shown a tendency
for journalists to place themselves on the left rather than the right of the
political centre (Johnstone et al. 1976; Weaver and Wilhoit 1986, 1996). International surveys have also found that journalists from Britain, Germany,
Italy, and Sweden prefer to place themselves slightly left of centre (Patterson
and Donsbach 1996). Other surveys have found that American journalists
more often identify themselves with Democratic rather than Republican
candidates (Lichter et al. 1991; Johnstone et al. 1976). British surveys have

found that 57 percent of journalists indicate their preference is for the Labour Party compared with 6 percent for the Conservative Party (Delano and Henningham 1995; Henningham 1996). Likewise, Australian surveys have found that journalists are twice as likely to identify with left-of-centre positions than with right-of-centre positions and they are more likely to vote for the Labour Party over the conservative Liberal Party (Henningham 1995, 1996).

Unlike the journalists studied in these international surveys, English-speaking Canadian journalists are just as likely to place themselves on the right as on the left of the political centre. Twenty-nine percent of English-speaking Canadian journalists describe themselves as moderately right wing, compared with 31 percent who say they are moderately left wing (17 percent of the public place themselves as moderately left wing). Slightly more journalists describe themselves as right wing (9 percent) compared with left wing (6 percent). None of the journalists in the survey indicated that they were very left wing or very right wing. Even though English-speaking Canadian journalists place themselves more to the right than journalists do in other countries, they still see themselves as less right wing than the public sees itself. Typically, therefore, Canadian journalists also place themselves to the left of their audience.

In addition to placing themselves on the left-right spectrum, we asked journalists to place their immediate supervisor on the same scale. Thirty percent of all journalists identified their immediate supervisor as moderately right wing, but 41 percent of the self-described moderately right-wing journalists placed their supervisor as moderately right wing. More than half (56 percent) of the self-described right-wing journalists gave their supervisors the same position. In contrast, left-wing journalists placed their supervisors to the right of themselves. Two-thirds of left-wing journalists placed their immediate supervisors as moderately left wing, and 42 percent of the moderately left-wing journalists placed their supervisors as moderately right wing. There seemed to be a significant amount of both ideological cohesion and ideological moderation within Canadian newsrooms, with no one adopting an extreme political position for themselves or for their supervisors.

The chief problem with ideological self-descriptions is that they can often be at the mercy of political correctness. Journalism does have an underlying or tacit commitment to objectivity, so it should not come as a surprise that journalists are unwilling to place themselves at either extreme of the political spectrum. Within this broad middle range, American and international research has shown that journalists tend to vote for liberal or social democratic parties. In order to see if this generalization applied to Canadian journalists as well and if their position was significantly different from that of the general public, we asked a standard survey question: "If a provincial election were being held in your province today, which provincial party would you vote for?" Two findings stand out. First, English-speaking journalists were more likely than the public to say that they "didn't know" who they would vote for (34 percent versus 23 percent). Second, the only party that the journalists were more willing than the general public to support was the NDP (11 percent compared with 9 percent). The public was slightly more likely to vote Conservative (18 percent) than journalists (15 percent); the Liberal vote was nearly identical and not a statistically significant difference (28 percent public; 30 percent journalists).

Because of the varying importance of ideology within the provincial system, it is difficult to disentangle local issues from ideology on this question. In turning to the federal arena, we asked, "For which party did you vote for in this past spring's [1997] federal election?" Here the differences between the English-speaking public and journalists are more pronounced. Compared with the journalist sample, the general population was more willing to support the Conservative, Liberal, and Reform parties. The only political party that the journalists said they voted for in higher proportion than the public was the NDP. Eight percent of the public indicated that they voted NDP; 20 percent of the journalists claimed this to be their choice. At the other end of the political spectrum, 15 percent of the public said they voted Reform, and 12 percent of journalists gave Reform their vote.

The difference in the English-speaking sample is even more striking when CBC journalists were compared with journalists in the private sector. CBC radio reporters were more likely than private journalists, or even their counterparts in television, to vote NDP. Fourteen percent of private journalists indicated that they voted for the NDP in the last federal election campaign, but 40 percent of CBC radio journalists said that they voted NDP. In striking contrast, only 8 percent of CBC television reporters said they voted NDP in the last election. Because of the small sample size of the CBC journalists, it is difficult to say whether this finding is representative of all

CBC radio journalists. The results as presented are not statistically significant and therefore we cannot rule out a chance variation for the distribution of these data. However, it is important to note that the support for the NDP comes primarily from the radio rather than the television journalists. By the same token, the aforementioned support for the Reform Party came chiefly from private-sector journalists, and to a lesser extent from CBC-TV journalists. Four percent of CBC radio journalists said they voted Reform, compared with 8 percent of CBC-TV journalists and 16 percent of private-sector journalists.

Placing oneself on a left–right scale and describing voting behaviour does not exhaust the complex question of ideological belief or party allegiance. Moreover, the traditional conceptions of right and left or conservative and liberal do not always take into account the values and ideas people hold about public policy issues, particularly in a postmaterialist environment, nor the intensity with which they hold them. In order to obtain a more complete picture of the sentiments and beliefs that underlie journalists' voting decisions or the journalists' self-placements on left–right scales, we asked respondents a series of specific questions on different social, economic, and national political issues.

The questions asked in this survey were informed by the series of questions developed by Ron Inglehart in his postmaterialism studies. Inglehart and others who study the changing of values in Western democracies developed an array of questions designed to document those changes. The measurement used most often by Inglehart and his colleagues to gauge materialist/postmaterialist tendencies is a two-question sequence that is usually worded to ask respondents to consider "what this country's goals should be for the next 10 or 15 years" and to choose from one of four items labelled as "most important in the long run." Those choices are: (a) maintaining order in the nation; (b) giving the people more say in important government decisions; (c) fighting rising prices; and (d) protecting freedom of speech. Respondents are then asked to select their second most important item. Respondents selecting (a) and (c) are classified as materialist and those selecting (b) and (d) are classified as postmaterialists. Those selecting different combinations are considered "mixed."

This approach has been the subject of many methodological analyses and criticisms. The most important in our mind is that the relative salience of these issues has varied substantially since the questions were first administered in the early 1970s (Clarke and Dutt 1991). As Clarke, Dutt, and Rapkin argue, "When unemployment becomes the dominant concern and inflation is no longer a salient feature of the economic context, respondents tend to eschew the prices item, while being forced by the question format to choose among the remaining three themes" (1997, 21). Historical changes since the 1970s have moved the goalposts or altered the issue space and, in any event, have diminished the comparability of the results, even though the same measure was used.

Rather than use the standard battery of questions that was developed a generation ago in an economic period of high inflation and high unemployment, we tailored our questions to reflect economic, social, and national issues that are part of the current milieu. While this makes our results more difficult to compare with other surveys, it means that our results should be easier to interpret. Since the values of journalists are one part of this study, we chose to narrow the number and type of questions. As a consequence, our questions are not identical to Inglehart's. We did, however, pose the same questions in the same order to both journalists and the general population.

Economic Issues

On economic issues, journalists differ little from the general population. We took the five questions that dealt with ideological issues surrounding the economic system and created an index of economic conservatism. Here we wanted to measure the extent to which journalists differ from the general population in their support of capitalism over communism. Using the combined mean score of the five economic questions in the English-speaking sample, journalists measured slightly more economically conservative than the public; on the five-item economic scale the general population had a mean score of 2.0215 and the journalists had a mean score of 2.1154.[3] Using the *t*-test, which examines the standard error of the difference in means, we find that the slight differences in the means scores for journalists and the general public are not statistically significant (Bryman and Cramer 1990, 6). In other words, we cannot reject the hypothesis that the public and journalists effectively mirror each other on the questions regarding capitalism and communism, and on the issue of public debt.

When English-speaking CBC journalists' scores are tabulated separately from private-sector journalists, however, a statistically significant difference does emerge. CBC journalists' mean score is 2.2750, placing their views on capitalism and the economy at the left-of-centre position. That score is statistically significant on a two-tailed t-test at the $p > 0.002$ level. In contrast, the mean score for private-sector journalists is 2.0156, a figure not statistically different from that of the general population. The conclusions to be drawn from this statistical analysis are first, that private-sector journalists are more likely to have views similar to the general public on economic issues, and second, that those opinions lie at the centre of the political spectrum.

Private-sector journalists indicate the same or stronger opinions on the desirability of capitalism, free markets, and private property compared with the public. Half of private-sector journalists and 39 percent of the general population think it is "extremely desirable" to have free markets and the right to own private property. In contrast, only 22 percent of CBC journalists said that it was "extremely desirable" to have free markets and capitalism.

Of the economic questions, the one instance where journalists scored more liberal than the general population was on the question of the debate on communism in the former Soviet Union. Here, half of the population of English-speaking journalists (50 percent) thought that communism in the former Soviet Union "may have been a good idea, but was wrecked by bad leadership" compared with 25 percent of the general population. Moreover, only 12 percent of the journalists describe the system under the Soviets as "essentially evil and unworkable" compared with 26 percent of the general population. At the same time, 2 percent of the general population thought that communism was "basically a good system," but no English-speaking journalist was willing to support the statement.

On more technical economic questions, English-speaking journalists and the general population are in agreement. Economist and Nobel laureate Milton Friedman has shown that, over the long term, there is no relationship between low inflation and high unemployment. Despite his evidence and the widespread acceptance of his arguments among economists, the popular belief in a relationship between inflation and unemployment persists. On the question of the trade-off between low inflation and unemployment, both English-speaking journalists and the general population typically agree that it is "somewhat true" that a trade-off exists. Eight percent of the general population and 10 percent of the journalists questioned thought that it was not at all true. Similarly on the question about the national debt, both the general public (67 percent) and journalists (61 percent) said that the problem is huge and fixing it should be made a top priority. One quarter (24 percent) of the general public and one-quarter (25 percent) of the journalist population thought that the problem had been exaggerated by right-wing interests. There are no statistically significant differences between the two groups. With both questions the two groups are willing to accept that the debt is a huge problem, and they both accept the economic fallacy that low inflation brings high unemployment. This dichotomy will be discussed in further detail when we examine the way the media report on economic issues.

Journalists might toy with the ideal of communism, but most English-speaking journalists are willing to concede that capitalist economies, competition, and private property bring more wealth, freedom, and better health to the largest number of people in society. Five percent of the journalists and 10 percent of the general population said that statement was completely true; 28 percent of journalists and 26 percent of the general population said there was "a lot of truth" to it. The largest percentage of both the general population (46 percent) and journalists (61 percent) picked the middle option that there was "some truth" to the statement. Although it does not reflect unanimous agreement with the opinion that capitalist economies offer the best solutions to material well-being, more endorsed capitalism than rejected it.

On one final economic issue the English-speaking journalists, by an overwhelming margin, thought that wealth was created more by hard work, education, and personal responsibility than by the power of governments and corporations. In this instance, agreement between the general population and journalists was almost complete, with 85 percent of journalists and 82 percent of the general population favouring what might be termed the personal responsibility option. The only difference in these findings is the strength with which respondents hold their opinions. More than three-quarters (78 percent) of the general population who said that hard work, education, and personal responsibility created wealth felt strongly about it.

In contrast, 58 percent of journalists who took the same point of view said that they felt strongly about it.

On economic issues, the journalists in aggregate favour capitalism over communism. In this respect, Noam Chomsky's view that journalists are sympathetic to capitalism has some merit. Journalists agree that the debt is an important issue, and they also believe that there is a trade-off between low inflation and employment. Moreover, they do so more than the general population.

Social Issues
To compare journalists with the general population on social issues, we asked a standard series of questions concerning the degree to which certain groups deserve respect in society. The responses were placed on a seven-point scale where 1 means the group deserves "no more respect than today" and 7 indicates the group deserves "a lot more respect than today." Because of the complexity of the variables, we used factor analysis, a statistical technique designed to indicate the existence of fundamental but unobtrusive variables or "factors." Basically, factor analysis lines up an array of responses to a series of questions and indicates the existence of underlying values linking the several questions. That is, it groups questions inductively into categories on the basis of actual responses rather than on the basis of pre-established categories. Factor analysis has been likened to a light rotating through a fog at the top of a lighthouse: you don't know what the light will pick up in the gloom until you turn it on and discover what "factors" are out there. Moreover, since the factors do not come with pre-given names, the analyst has to provide them.

On the basis of the issues with which we are concerned, the response patterns, the factors, might be called traditional/progressive or materialist/postmaterialist. When we analyze the English-speaking sample data dealing with social groups, for example, we find distinct differences that reflect progressive and traditional social values. The general population shows more of a mixed pattern on traditional/progressive scale, but the journalists' opinion clusters or "loads" more strongly on the progressive component. Among the general population, attitudes toward feminists, environmentalists, Aboriginal leaders, and academics who oppose American influence are grouped within a dimension we have labelled "progressive." Attitudes toward feminists and pro-choice groups are not strongly related to this factor.

In contrast, the factor loadings for the English-speaking journalist population were strongest in attitudes toward environmentalists, feminists, pro-choice groups, Aboriginal leaders, and academics who oppose American influence. Overall, these factors loaded more heavily for the journalists than for the population as a whole, indicative of a more consistent structure of attitudes among the journalists. Attitudes toward REAL Women, married couples, and pro-life groups load heavily on a second dimension, which we have labelled "traditional." Comparing scores on the two components between the two groups shows that journalists have higher factor loadings among the "progressive beliefs" than among "traditional beliefs," which indicates a higher level of attitudinal consistency, coherence, or "constraint." Thus, English-speaking journalists appear to conceptualize politics and political issues at a higher level of abstraction than the general public, leading to greater distinction between progressive and traditional issue perspectives.

One consequence of greater ideological consistency among Canadian journalists is that they may be more inclined to advocate polarized positions. The progressive attitude of English-speaking journalists can be seen more clearly when one contrasts their views on abortion with those of the general population. When asked whether a woman has both a moral and legal right to terminate her pregnancy, more than half (53 percent) of the journalists, but only slightly over one-third (36 percent) of the general population, say that they "highly agreed." In addition, 19 percent of the journalists and 16 percent of the general population say that they "agreed." The same proportion of journalists and the public indicate that they "somewhat agreed" with the statement. At the other end of the scale only 3 percent of journalists but 14 percent of the public say that they "highly disagreed" with the statement. There are no statistically significant differences between university graduates and the rest of the general population on this question. This corroborates anecdotal evidence from the United States that has found journalists to be more likely to be pro-choice than pro-life, and much more so than the general public (Eastland 1997).

One of the most striking differences between the English-speaking public and the journalists is on the issue of gays and lesbians. To evoke sentiments concerning homosexuality we asked whether "the rights of gays or homo-sexuals receive too much, somewhat much, or too little attention?" Slightly more than half of the English-speaking public (52 percent) but only 4 per-cent of the English-speaking journalists think that these groups receive "too much" attention. A further 24 percent of the public and 35 percent of the journalists think that these groups receive "somewhat much" attention. The combined total on the "much" side for the public is 76 percent, and 39 percent for journalists. Sixteen percent of the public but 29 percent of jour-nalists think that the rights of gays and lesbians receive too little attention. Not surprisingly, then, 4 percent of the general public and 29 percent of the journalists think the rights of gays and lesbians receive an appropriate amount of attention (the midpoint on a seven-point scale). There are no statistical differences between university-educated Canadians and the general popula-tion on this question.

English-speaking journalists are supportive of the capitalist system in gen-eral, which indicates a basic materialist disposition, but on social issues they provide a stronger postmaterialist orientation. Moreover, English-language journalist opinions on social issues are stronger on the postmaterialist scale than were the opinions of the general population. More important, these opinions are more strongly held than are opinions held by people in the general population who had obtained similar levels of education. Therefore we are led to conclude that journalists' opinions are different from the non-journalist general population and different from élite opinion as well. Fur-ther, though journalists accept the capitalist system, they are more likely to support new social movements promoting the rights of gays, Aboriginal peoples, and women. In other words, journalists as a group may or may not be fiscal conservatives but they definitely are not social conservatives.

National Unity

The postmaterialist paradigm includes variables on regime threat. Many of these questions relate to how respondents view authority (Nevitte 1996, 41); others, especially American researchers, have examined the concept of re-gime threat (Lichter et al. 1991, 47). Cold War sentiments, which once mat-tered a great deal, have become generally outdated since the Berlin Wall fell; indeed, one could make the argument that Cold War issues have never been as important to Canadians as to Americans. On the other hand, national unity issues have been of great importance to Canadians, and they are what we chose to examine as a measurement of regime threat.

First, we asked both journalists and the general public whether they saw themselves mainly as Canadians or mainly as residents of the province they lived in. For both the English-speaking public and the journalists, there was an overwhelming response in favour of seeing themselves as mainly Canadian. Ninety-one percent of the public and 89 percent of journalists saw themselves mainly as Canadian.

There was less agreement on the questions regarding Quebec separatist politicians. Respondents were asked whether they saw separatist or sovereigntist politicians in Quebec as "highly constructive," "somewhat constructive," "somewhat destructive," or "very destructive." Both the English-speaking public and the journalist populations see Quebec separatist politicians on the destructive side of the scale, but the public holds stronger views than do the journalists. Fifty-eight percent of the public and 45 percent of the journalists identify Quebec separatist politicians as "very destructive." There are more journalists willing to say that Quebec separatist politicians are "somewhat destructive" than are members of the public.

On the subject of partition of Quebec, English-speaking journalists and the general public have strikingly different levels of general knowledge. Three-quarters of the general public (75 percent) say they recall "hearing something in the news about the possibility that the territory of Quebec could be partitioned or divided if Quebec became a separate country, with some land going with an independent Quebec and other land staying in Canada"; almost all the journalists (97 percent) indicated that they had. A majority of both the general (70 percent) and journalist (84 percent) populations indicate that regions in Quebec should have the right to decide whether to go with Quebec or stay in Canada, but here journalists led public opinion.

To summarize this analysis of the attitudes of anglophone journalists on economic, social, and national unity issues: they are ambivalent. The anglophone journalists concede that capitalism and free markets bring about the greatest wealth to the greatest number of people but they also believe that communism was basically a good idea that was wrecked by bad leadership.

They are more cohesive on the progressive scale than is the general population on such social issues as abortion and gay rights and they are less likely to be supportive of pro-life groups, married people who make every effort to stay together, and traditional women's groups. On national issues, they are less likely to be critical of separatist politicians in Quebec than the general public, but more likely than the general public to support the partition of regions of Quebec if Quebec were to separate from Canada. We now turn to francophone responses.

FRENCH-SPEAKING MEDIA PERSONNEL

Demographics

Unlike the anglophone journalists, francophone journalists have more in common demographically with their audience. Both groups are typically married or are living with a partner, both have about one child living at home, and a plurality of both groups indicate that they do not belong to any religion. Of those who do belong to a religious denomination, almost all called themselves Roman Catholic. Where there are differences between francophone journalists and their audience, however, those differences are highly significant. French-speaking journalists are, for example, older than the public, much more likely to be university educated, and less likely definitely to believe in God.

Eighty percent of journalists hold a university or post-graduate degree compared with only 21 percent of the general population. As we found in the English-speaking general population sample, 44 percent of the francophone general population hold a high school diploma or less. One-third (35 percent) of the francophone general population has some college or university. In contrast, only 2 percent of the journalists had high school education or less, and 18 percent indicate that they have had some college or university education.

There are no statistically significant differences between the marital status of the general public and journalists, although francophone journalists are slightly more likely to be married than is the general population. Almost half of the journalists (47 percent) and one-third (34.3 percent) of the public are married. Both groups have the same proportion of people living with a partner. The public has a slightly higher proportion than do the journalists of individuals who indicate that they have never been married (32 percent versus 29 percent, respectively).

Again, the tests of significance show no statistical differences between the two groups. However, the distribution of children living at home produces some anomalies in the francophone sample. While more members of the general population have no children living at home, they also are more likely to have large families. Thus, though both samples have the median number of children living at home as one, the journalist sample has a smaller range of children than does the public.

Similar to the English-speaking sample, French-speaking journalists are most likely to be in their thirties and forties. Thirty-one percent of journalists are in their thirties compared with 25 percent of the general public. An additional 40 percent of journalists are in their forties compared with 25 percent of the general population. This finding reveals a significant change in the composition of journalists today from their profile during the 1980s. A survey taken for the Royal Commission on Newspapers found that "journalists and managers of the major French language dailies, are, on the average, younger than those of the major English-language dailies. The high number of journalists in their 40s and 50s who leave the profession is, in fact, one of the tragedies of the Québec press" (Gagnon 1981, 29). Clearly this aspect of the demographic profile of French-speaking journalists has changed over the past quarter-century.

Our survey also measured the spiritual profile of francophone Canadians. A higher percentage of journalists than members of the general population indicate that they have no religious denomination. Half of the general population (50 percent) indicate that they have no religious affiliation, but two-thirds of journalists (66 percent) eschew religious organizations. Of those who indicate they belong to a religion, 92 percent of the public and 95 percent of journalists call themselves Catholic.

As we found in the English sample, French journalists who describe themselves as Catholic are less likely to attend religious services than the public. Although the population in Quebec overall has lower levels of church attendance than non-Quebec residents, francophone journalists have the lowest attendance rates of all. As Bibby (1987, 20) found, Catholic Church attendance in Canada has had no greater decline than in Quebec. Thirty-eight percent of Quebec Catholics attended mass twice a month or more in 1985. This was a 50 percentage-point decline from the rates seen in 1965. We found that one-quarter (24 percent) of Catholic journalists attend mass regularly, which provides some evidence that, although on the surface Quebec journalists are similar to their public, in fact they lead the decline in traditional practices and values.

Some of the most striking differences between francophone journalists and their audiences are found when we asked respondents the extent to which they believe in God. A majority (61 percent) of the public declare that they "definitely believe," but less than one-third (31 percent) of journalists make this assertion. Journalists are more likely to hedge their bets, saying that they "probably do" (27 percent). Moreover, 18 percent say that they "probably don't" and 15 percent indicate that they "definitely don't" believe in God.

Francophone journalism at the élite level is male-dominated. Eighty percent of our sample is male compared with an even distribution of men and women in the general population survey.

Unlike the English-speaking sample, where journalists are only somewhat more likely to consume alcoholic beverages than the general population, francophone journalists clearly drink more than the general public. The mean number of days a week that members of the public have beer or alcoholic beverages is 1.57; it is nearly twice that much for the journalist sample, at 2.63. Incidentally, this is also higher than the rate of alcoholic consumption among English-speaking journalists. There is a higher frequency of people in the general public who have no alcoholic beverages in a typical week than in the journalist sample (43 percent compared with 18 percent). At the other extreme there is a greater proportion of journalists who indicate that they regularly drink several days a week (15 percent) compared with the general population (1 percent).

When we examine only educated francophones compared with the French-speaking journalists, we find that the differences cannot be explained by education alone. Journalists have decidedly different demographic characteristics than their similarly educated counterparts. Although there are only two findings that are statistically significant, a number of things indicated in Figure 4.2 stand out. First, 54 percent of the male population is university educated compared with the 80 percent rate in the journalist sample. The public is less likely to be married than the journalist sample (32

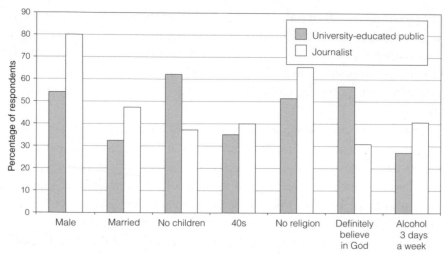

Figure 4.2   Social background of French-speaking educated public and
journalists, December 1997-January 1998

percent compared with 47 percent). The educated French-speaking population is almost twice as likely to be childless than our journalist sample. This
difference is statistically significant. Journalists are slightly more likely to be
in their forties than is their public. Most striking is the finding that on the
question of belief in God, more than half (57 percent) of the educated general public say that they "definitely" believe in God compared with the 31
percent of journalists. Journalists are also more likely to consume alcoholic
beverages more than three days a week than are their audience.

   The above findings do not show francophone journalists leading the
general public on postmaterialist demographics to the same degree as their
English-speaking colleagues, but where they do differ, those differences are
statistically significant.

Ideology

As was indicated above, the effect of demographic characteristics on individual behaviour or individual belief cannot be estimated a priori for the
perfectly obvious reason that demographic data characterize groups, and
attitudes belong to individuals. After the fact, however, they can provide
some useful empirical insights. The demographic profile of francophone
journalists seems to be closer to the French-speaking public than was the fit

between English-speaking journalists and their public. It also turns out that francophone journalists are closer to their audience on the political spectrum than are English-speaking journalists. Second, unlike their English-speaking counterparts, French-speaking journalists are more likely to place themselves on the left of the political spectrum than the right, and they are more likely to do so than their public. Eleven percent of both the public and francophone journalists place themselves as "left wing." This is twice the proportion that so declared themselves in the English-speaking population. However, 36 percent of francophone journalists and 19 percent of the public describe themselves as "moderately left wing." Again, these figures are higher for both groups than in the English-speaking sample. Moreover, francophones are more likely to place themselves in the middle of the political spectrum than is the case with the English population. One-quarter of francophone journalists (26 percent) and one-fifth (19 percent) of the public consider their political views to be at the "centre" of the political spectrum. Unlike the English-speaking sample, French-speaking journalists are less likely to place themselves as either "moderately right wing" or "right wing": only 9 percent of the journalists, but 15 percent of the public, place themselves as "moderately right wing"; similarly, only 7 percent of journalists, and 10 percent of the public identify themselves as "right wing." Further, while 3 percent of the public consider themselves to be "very right wing," no francophone journalist made that claim.

The results of self-descriptions on the political spectrum are not statistically significant, but differences in provincial election support are. The largest difference between the public and the francophone journalist population is between those who indicated that they "didn't know" which provincial party they would support. Almost half (47 percent) the journalists, but about one-quarter (27 percent) of the public are undecided on provincial party support. This rises to almost two-thirds (61 percent) for journalists and one-third (33 percent) for the general public when the category "none of these" is included with the "don't know." Whether these numbers truly reflect the indecisiveness of journalists may be questionable. It does seem to be true, however, that francophone journalists are less likely to declare their support for the Parti Québécois than are the public. Only 11 percent of journalists indicate that they would vote Parti Québécois, while more than one-third (37 percent) of the public indicate their preference is Péquiste. In fact, francophone journalists are almost evenly spilt between those who say they support the Liberals and those who say they support the Parti Québécois. Incidentally, members of the public with university degrees are strongest in their support for the Parti Québécois, giving the party 41 percent of their support.

Similarly, on the federal level francophone journalists are more likely to support the Liberals than the Bloc Québécois. One-fifth of the journalists (20 percent) declare themselves to be Liberal supporters, compared with 15 percent who support the Bloc. In contrast, the general public is more likely to support the Bloc at 33 percent, compared with 24 percent who favour the Liberals. Where the journalists particularly differentiate themselves from their public is in their support for the NDP. On both the provincial and federal level, francophone journalists are more likely to support the NDP than are members of the public. On the provincial level 6 percent of journalists compared with only 1 percent of the general public say they would vote NDP. On the federal level, support of the general public for the NDP remains unchanged, but journalists' support increases to 11 percent. These findings are statistically significant. The federal election numbers also show fewer journalists to be interested in the federal election campaign. While 20 percent indicate that they do not know how they voted in the last election, a further 20 percent say that they "didn't vote."

The implications of this finding are puzzling. At the same time as journalists indicate they are not particularly strong supporters of the Bloc, an even larger number indicate that they are not interested in federal elections at all. In contrast, the general public is both more interested in federal elections and more likely to vote for a sovereigntist party to represent the province. The educated general public differs substantially from the journalist population and strongly supports the Bloc Québécois at 35 percent. This may well indicate that francophone journalists have already disengaged their political identity from the rest of the country, a question we will explore in greater detail when we examine issues surrounding Quebec nationalism.

Economic Issues

Despite the relatively strong support for the NDP, as a group francophone journalists are also generally enamoured of the capitalist system. Journalists and the public show similar levels of support for the desirability of free markets. The mean scores for the economic index show no statistical difference between French-speaking journalists and the francophone public. The mean score for the public is 2.0752 and the mean score for journalists is 2.0394. There are no statistical differences between these two populations running the independent *t*-test. On economic issues, then, both populations balance their views around the centre of the economic political spectrum. While in the English-speaking sample there were significant differences in response profiles depending on whether the journalists worked for the private or public sector, no such differences existed in the French-speaking sample. The mean score for Radio-Canada journalists is 2.1493, while the mean score for private-sector journalists is 1.9543. While francophone CBC journalists appear to be slightly more economically liberal and private journalists more economically conservative, these differences are not statistically significant, probably because of the small sample size.

One-quarter (26 percent) of francophone journalists and almost one-quarter (23 percent) of their public agree that free markets and capitalism are "extremely desirable." A further 31 percent of the journalists and 41 percent of the public think it is "very desirable." One-third of the journalists (35 percent) and one-quarter (25 percent) of the general public think it is "somewhat desirable." Very few think it is "not really desirable" or "not at all desirable." As was the case with the English-speaking sample, there are no statistically significant differences between the two groups on this question.

There are, however, statistically significant differences between the French-speaking public and francophone journalists regarding their views on communism. A full quarter of the general public (27 percent) think that communism under the former Soviets was "essentially evil and unworkable," but less than one-fifth (18 percent) of the journalists hold the same view. Sixteen percent of the public think that Soviet communism was "at least partly evil and unworkable" but almost one-quarter of the journalists (24 percent) hold that view. The real differences emerge in the view that communism "may have been a good idea, but was wrecked by bad leadership." Only 17 percent of the public is of this opinion, compared with almost half (47 percent) of the journalists. The view of the public is more evenly dispersed, with most respondents thinking it was a bad system, but some acknowledging that it might, after all, have been a good system. In contrast, journalists are more likely to adopt the middle position and have less range in their opinions about communism as a whole.

This trend is carried through in the next question, concerning attitudes toward capitalism, wealth, and freedom. The French-speaking public is distributed almost in a bell curve with respect to the degree to which individuals agreed with the statement that capitalism brings about greater wealth and freedom, whereas the journalists are more likely to support the statement. One-fifth (20 percent) think there is "a lot of truth" to the statement, and two-thirds think there was "some truth" to it.

Remarkably, as is the case in the English sample, francophone journalists and their public alike think to some extent that there is a trade-off between unemployment and inflation. Only 9 percent of both the francophone journalists and their public are emphatic that it is "not true at all." There are some statistical differences in the degree of support for the statement between the two groups, but both groups believe there is a trade-off. The one economic question that commands agreement regardless of the group is the issue of debt. Very few Canadians, regardless of their education, language, or occupation, think that the debt is not an important priority. Of the French-speaking population, 71 percent of the public and 64 percent of the journalists think that the size of the debt is important. These are very similar numbers to the opinions held by English-speaking populations.

On the last economic issue, journalists are more likely to agree that hard work, education, and personal responsibility are key elements in individual success. Eighty-one percent of the francophone journalists hold this view, about the same as their anglophone colleagues, but only 63 percent of the public is of the same opinion. Unlike the English-speaking sample, however, there are no differences in the degree of support for the position. Among those who declare hard work, education, and personal responsibility to be the key factors to success, three-quarters of both groups feel strongly about it.

Unlike the English-speaking sample, the francophone journalist population does not always lead the opinion of the educated population. On the left-right questions, whether capitalism brings wealth, whether there is a trade-off between unemployment and inflation, and whether the debt is an important matter, there are no statistical differences between the educated francophones and the journalist samples. However, on the question of Soviet communism, 40 percent of the educated sample indicate that they think it was "essentially evil and unworkable," but only 18 percent of journalists do. At the same time, however, the university-educated public views the power of governments as having a greater impact on wealth creation than hard work and personal responsibility. This contrast indicates a significant division in perspective between journalists and the better educated in their audience.

The comparison of ideology between the French-speaking general population and the journalists echoes the findings in the English-speaking sample. Journalists are indeed an ambivalent lot, but so too is the francophone public. While francophone journalists tend to support federal and provincial New Democrats and to consider themselves moderately left wing, they also find free markets and capitalism desirable, are willing to agree that capitalism brings on the greatest wealth and freedom, but also admit support for communism. They may believe that there is a trade-off between unemployment and inflation, but they are aware of the debt and consider it a real problem for the nation. To complicate matters further, the journalists also strongly believe that hard work, education, and personal responsibility create wealth – and they believe this more strongly than the public.

Social Issues
On social issues, factor analysis yields very different results from those obtained from the English-speaking sample. While pro-choice groups, environmentalists, and Aboriginal leaders score higher on the progressive component for francophone journalists than for the public, so too do REAL Women and married couples. In the case of Aboriginal leaders, the public rank them on the bottom of the scale, but they placed third on the journalist factor loads.

Francophone journalists are less hostile to traditional women's groups as well as to traditional beliefs such as the desirability of keeping married couples together. At the same time, however, they are not supportive of feminists or pro-life groups. It appears that francophone journalists distrust equally groups presented as being positioned on either end of the political or social policy spectrum.

In contrast to the English-speaking population, the French-speaking population does not place seemingly disparate groups in different dimensions or factors. Indeed, in the general population the only groups that did not load heavily on the first dimension were married couples, pro-life groups, and

Aboriginal leaders. Labelling the first dimension "progressive" as we did in the English sample appears to be misplaced when one examines the placement of the socially conservative REAL Women along the same dimension as pro-choice groups. Apart from this anomaly, the other categories in the dimension make intuitive sense, with feminists and pro-choice groups strongly related on this factor.

Francophone journalists, however, place pro-choice groups, environmentalists, Aboriginal leaders, REAL Women, and married couples in the dimension we called "progressive." This indicates that the underlying value orientation of French-speaking journalists cannot be labelled easily in the progressive/traditional dichotomy that seems to fit anglophone journalists. In fact, only pro-life loaded on the dimension we called "traditional," despite the fact that REAL Women, which has similar tenets as pro-life groups, loaded on the "progressive" dimension. This gives us some concern about whether francophones either were unclear on what the group REAL Women stands for or do not have the same conceptualization of such groups as the English sample. That the journalist population loaded these factors more heavily than did the general population indicates that francophone journalists do not conceptualize political groups at a higher level of abstraction compared with either the general public or the English sample. For the francophone population as a whole, and for journalists in particular, there seems to be little distinction between progressive and traditional issue perspectives.

On the issue of abortion rights, francophone journalists display a more consistently progressive attitude than do members of their public. Although the public is supportive of REAL Women as well as of feminists, they are disdainful of pro-choice organizations and more supportive of pro-life organizations. At the same time, however, 33 percent "highly agree" that a woman has a moral and legal right to abortion. In contrast, journalists who rank pro-choice groups high and pro-life groups low on the progressive factor are more consistent in their abortion stance. Almost half (47 percent) of francophone journalists "highly agree" that a woman has a moral and legal right to an abortion. A further 33 percent "agreed" and only 2 percent "somewhat disagreed." Although the majority of the general population is also in the "agreed" category, a substantial number fell into either the "somewhat disagreed" or "highly disagreed" camps. There are no significant differences between the journalists and university-educated francophones on this issue.

On the question of gays and lesbians, the public offers the most support, not the journalists. Seventy-three percent of francophone journalists think that gays and lesbians receive "somewhat much" attention (the answer between "too much" and "too little" attention) compared with 22 percent of the public. While no journalist indicated a belief that gays and lesbians receive an appropriate amount of attention (the midpoint of a seven-point scale), one-fifth of the public did choose this option. There are also slight, but statistically significant, differences between the journalists and university graduates on this question, with university graduates reflecting the views of the general public.

To sum up these findings: the English-speaking sample has more in common with the postmaterialist pattern than the francophone sample. Both the public and the journalists present anomalous results. The French-speaking population has a mixture of tolerance for both feminists and traditional women's groups and is disdainful of both pro-life and pro-choice groups, but at the same time is supportive of abortion rights. While the francophone population in general has mixed views on homosexuals, it is the journalists who think they receive a slightly disproportionate amount of attention. While some differences between the general public and the journalists can be explained by education, others such as homosexual issues cannot. So, while the English-speaking journalists lead public opinion on postmaterialist values, the same cannot be said for the French-speaking population. Neither the public nor the journalists score high on postmaterialist values.

National Unity

Probably the single largest difference between French- and English-speaking Canadians is their views on national unity and Quebec sovereignty. The general public in Quebec is evenly split on whether they see themselves first as residents of the province or of the nation. In contrast, 60 percent of francophone journalists indicate that they see themselves as residents of the province before they see themselves as residents of Canada. While there are no statistically significant differences in the responses (again probably because of the small sample sizes), the journalists lead both the general public and university-educated French population.

Not surprisingly, both francophone journalists and the public, regardless of education, feel that Quebec separatist politicians are "somewhat constructive." While 16 percent of the public and 13 percent of the journalists think they are "highly constructive," one-fifth of both samples indicate that they are "somewhat destructive." Educated francophones are even more supportive of Quebec separatist politicians than are the journalists or the public.

The issue of Quebec partition is well known in all French-speaking samples. Ninety-eight percent of journalists and 79 percent of the public have heard of the possibility of Quebec being partitioned in the event of a "yes" vote in a Quebec referendum. Among those who are aware of the possibility of the partition of Quebec, there is a significant split between the journalists and the general population. Fifty-three percent of the general public think that regions of Quebec should be allowed to decide whether to go with Quebec or remain with Canada, but only 29 percent of the journalists feel the same way. A full 56 percent of francophone journalists think that regions of Quebec do not have that right compared with 40 percent of the general public. While educated francophones are more in keeping with the journalists' opinion, it is journalists who have stronger beliefs in this regard.

In sum, the analysis of the French-speaking population shows far fewer differences between the public and the journalists than does the analysis of their English-speaking colleagues. Moreover, when differences exist they tend to reflect educational rather than occupational factors.

We have shown that journalists have values and at times those values are different from the publics they report to. The question remains, however, whether those values creep into the news that is reported on a daily basis. Can journalists' opinions influence the tone and direction of newspaper and television coverage of economics, national unity, and social issues? In other words, journalists have opinions, but do those opinions matter? This question will be examined in depth in the three chapters that examine media content of those specific issues. Before we turn to such data, we must deal with the opposite question: Does ownership matter? In the next chapter we discuss the questions from the survey of journalists on what they say the role of owners has had on their work, and also, their views on the biases of other news outlets.

CHAPTER 5

THE NEWSROOM
AND CONTENT ANALYSIS

THE NEWSROOM

In this chapter we describe how the values discussed in the previous two chapters translate in the newsroom. As noted earlier, it has been a long-standing interest of academic media analysts as well as of ideologically motivated media critics and royal commissioners to express their concern, and indeed their anxieties, over concentration of ownership of media outlets in Canada. The assumption underlying these sentiments is that a small number of owners of a large number of media outlets will influence news coverage, reduce the plurality of voices in the public square, and thus undermine democracy itself. In Chapter 1, we argued first, on theoretical grounds, that newspapers must sell their product and so cannot afford to offend their readers on a daily basis; thus, they will reflect (more or less) the views and interests of their readers. Second, we reported the results of an empirical analysis of the "before" and "after" content of the Hollinger-owned outlets. There were changes, but they were inconsistent and many were not statistically significant. Although we have not come across any replication of that study since the purchase of Southam by CanWest Global, there is simply no reason to think that the results would be different.

In this chapter and the subsequent chapters, we are going to examine not just the *output* of newspapers but the internal dynamics of the newsroom. Given the well-known political and economic views of the Hollinger CEO,

95

Conrad Black, and his sharply critical opinion of the work ethic, productivity, and politics of many journalists; and given the apparent accuracy of Black's perception of the broad configuration of journalists' political opinions, as described in the previous chapters, one may anticipate that many journalists might feel uncomfortable working for a Black-controlled paper. For example, in a 15 June 1998 *Maclean's* column Anthony Wilson-Smith mused, "And is it true, as Black insists, that he does not interfere with editorial decisions? He does not have to: everyone in Southam realizes − and discusses − the career implications of falling out of favour" (Wilson-Smith 1998b). Whether or not journalists actually feel under pressure from owners, whether owners can induce a "chilly climate" on otherwise red-hot reporters and columnists, has, in fact, never been determined in Canada by the straightforward method of asking them. The last part of our survey therefore asked journalists about their views on the newsroom and how ideology affected their work.

All journalists were asked a series of questions about the newsroom and about their views of both their superiors and other news organizations. The first thing to note is that there are no statistically significant differences between French- and English-speaking journalists on any of these questions. This is striking because there are a number of ideological issues where the two populations differ. We therefore analyzed the data not according to language but according to whether the journalists work in the private or the public sector. Here we did find differences, both in their opinions about each other as groups and in the perception of the environment in which they work. We will present the data in aggregate and highlight differences between journalists working in the private sector and those who work for the CBC/Radio-Canada.

There are only small differences, but they are statistically significant, between the private- and public-sector journalists on how they describe their immediate manager or supervisor. CBC journalists are more likely to describe their immediate supervisor as left wing than are private-sector journalists. Thirteen percent of CBC journalists describe their superiors as "left wing," whereas only 4 percent of private-sector journalists make the same evaluation of their supervisors. While 42 percent of CBC journalists place their supervisors as "moderately left wing," one-fifth (20 percent) of private-sector journalists place their supervisors as "moderately left wing." Instead, the description most often used of a private-sector manager, at 31 percent, is "moderately right wing." In contrast, only 13 percent of CBC journalists describe their supervisors as "moderately right wing."

Probably more telling in the perceptions of a supervisor's political ideology is where the respondents place themselves on the political spectrum. When we asked journalists to place their immediate supervisor, those journalists who call themselves left wing place supervisors to the right of themselves; those who call themselves right wing as well as those describing themselves in the middle place their supervisors on the same point as themselves in the political spectrum. More than half (55 percent) of the journalists who describe their own views as "left wing" place their immediate supervisor as "moderately left wing." Similarly, 44 percent of those journalists who describe themselves as "moderately left wing" place their supervisors as "moderately right wing." Those who are not sure of their own political ideology are equally as unsure of their supervisors'.

Clearly, some journalists do not feel that they have the same ideological beliefs as their immediate supervisors. The significant question, however, is whether that perception has any effect on how they do their jobs. When asked whether they have ever "sensed, where you presently work, any misgivings, reservations or criticisms about your own views or reporting on the left or right in politics," 67 percent of CBC journalists but 86 percent of private-sector journalists indicate that they have not. These differences are statistically significant at the 90 percent level. Ninety-six percent of CBC and 97 percent of private-sector journalists indicate that they have not "been specifically told by a boss or colleagues that your political views were inappropriate in any way."

Part of the reason for this lack of conflict might be that journalists select, or are hired by, organizations that have like-minded management. To see if this is true, all journalists were asked questions about their perception of the political ideology of different news organizations in the country. The sequence of questions was rotated to ensure random responses. The base question asked journalists if those at a specific news outlet (in the case of Southam, before Conrad Black had majority control) "feel that they might fit the culture of their colleagues better if they highlighted the weaknesses or hypocrisies of business, political conservatives, or the right wing. So far as you can tell, is this: Totally true, Largely true, Somewhat true, Not really true, or

Not at all true?" An additional question reversed the categories for Southam (for the period once Black had majority control) and asked whether journalists felt that they might fit the culture of their colleagues better "if they highlighted views that are supportive of free market or conservative political ideas."

Considering how this question applies to CBC radio, 46 percent of the public-sector journalists indicate that it is "not true at all" that CBC has a specific position regarding markets compared with only 14 percent of private-sector journalists. One-quarter of CBC journalists said it is "not really true" compared with 33 percent of the private-sector journalists. At the same time 17 percent of CBC journalists admit that the statement is "somewhat true," compared with more than one-quarter (27 percent) of private-sector journalists. Interestingly, 8 percent of both CBC and private-sector journalists think the statement is "largely true," while an additional 2 percent of private-sector journalists say that it is "totally true." In other words, journalists outside CBC think that CBC is more likely to be critical of business and free markets than do journalists inside CBC.

A similar dichotomy emerges in the discussion of CBC-TV and Newsworld. Once again, 75 percent of CBC journalists disagree to some extent with the statement, for both CBC-TV and Newsworld. In contrast, almost half (46 percent) of private-sector journalists think that CBC-TV has a culture that is critical of business and 40 percent think the same for CBC Newsworld.

There is much more agreement in the statement regarding Southam before Conrad Black took over majority control of the corporation. While half (50 percent) of CBC journalists agree with the statement to some extent, more than one-third (35 percent) of private-sector journalists also agree. However, while only 13 percent of CBC journalists say that it was "not really true," 22 percent of private-sector journalists say the same. A large proportion of both types of journalists indicate that they "do not know" what the climate was before the takeover of Southam (29 percent, CBC; 34 percent, private).

Although many CBC journalists deny that CBC has a culture of criticizing the right, the same does not hold on the question of whether Southam, at the time of the survey, had a culture supportive of the right. On the question of whether Southam journalists would do better if they were supportive of the market, 29 percent of CBC journalists said that it was "largely true," compared with 13 percent of private-sector journalists. A further 21 percent of CBC and 30 percent of private journalists said that it was "somewhat true." About the same proportion of journalists denied the statement (17 percent), but only 6 percent of private-sector journalists denied it outright.

Journalists may have differing political views from their superiors, but those views do not translate into their being criticized or censored on the job. Journalists who work outside CBC are more likely to believe that CBC has an internal culture that is openly hostile to markets and the conservative economic agenda. At the same time, journalists both within the private sector and within CBC thought that the culture of Southam was supportive of markets and the conservative agenda. It is true that journalists do not believe that their political views have an impact on the way they report the news, but they do seem to self-select their news organizations. For example, CBC journalists, both French- and English-speaking, are more likely to be NDP supporters than journalists in any other news organization. More significant is the finding that those on the right feel more stifled than those on the left, regardless of where they work.

CONTENT ANALYSIS

The main question examined in this study is the extent to which the personal opinions and attitudes of journalists on public policy issues affect how the news is reported. Whatever the political culture of the newsroom may be, in principle that culture is distinct from the results of its operation, which is the actual news product. In order to make a persuasive case regarding the link between the opinions of journalists and the news produced, we must have a reliable way of measuring the output. This is what quantitative content analysis does. As indicated above, we conducted such a content analysis on three issue areas over the course of one year on a variety of newspapers as well as examples from television. This is not an exhaustive analysis of all the news organizations in the country, though it does give the flavour of the main and élite organizations. The reason why we can link journalist opinion with selected news coverage is in the nature of random sampling. The journalist survey was a random sample of journalists working in the major news organizations (apart from wire services) across the country. As such, the results can be generalized to journalists working in that area. When we select newspaper and television programs to content analyze, we are using a proxy for private and public media. The theory is that a random sample of journalists will be reflected in the news organizations of the major newspapers and television networks in the country.

Journalists are active and perceptive human beings, not passive or mechanical information-transmission devices. Or, as we observed earlier, news is the product of human agency, a transfiguration and mediation of events. It is self-evident in the sense that it follows from the nature of news production that the producers will influence the product. The question to be considered, thus, must be focused and refined. The issue is not "*Do* journalists influence news production?" but "Do journalists *have a greater influence on the news product* than other factors: day-to-day events, occupational routines, or ownership of the news media?" In the previous chapter we surveyed the opinions of Canadian journalists. In the preceding section of this chapter we noted the existence of factors within the newsroom that may influence the selection of stories, as well as other kinds of pressures journalists may feel from superiors. Finally, we asked journalists what they thought about the other major news organizations in the country.

Before indicating in detail the content analysis methods used in this study, it is necessary to deal with a preliminary question. Because journalists do not constitute the only source of information in a news story, perhaps the whole issue of looking at the opinions of journalists in the context of the news they report is misguided. After all, news stories result from the competition of various individuals and groups as well as ongoing events. How then, the objection may be made, can the personal opinions of journalists have any bearing on events or views over which they have no control?

We begin with the point, several times made, that news is produced, which does not mean that it is made up like a movie. It does mean, however, that journalists elicit and select their news sources to furnish them with particular opinions. Anyone who has been asked for his or her views by a journalist has experienced an occasion when a journalist asks a question in order to get a particular response. This may be to obtain a source quotation that affirms the journalist's view or it may serve as a counterbalance to an opinion of someone else. We will test the congruence between personal values disclosed by the journalist survey and the political values turned up by the content analyses.

Method

To test whether the value orientations of Canadian journalists influence news coverage, we conducted three content analyses on various television and newspaper outlets in the country. Content analysis is a technique that systematically classifies textual information (Holsti 1969). As communication scholars Bernard Berelson and Paul Lazarsfeld (1948, 5) define the procedure, "content analysis is a research technique for the objective, systematic, and quantitative description of manifest content of communication." Objectivity means "each step in the research process must be carried out on the basis of explicitly formulated rules and procedures" (Holsti 1981, 220). To ensure objectivity, research assistants, not the authors, were hired to devise code books and rule books to determine how to code stories, and to undertake the actual content analysis. The researchers developed and agreed upon all the rules in the study. These rules were used to train coders in analysis procedures as well as how to resolve disputed cases. "Systematic" means that the set, rule-defined procedure is equally applied to each part of the content being analyzed (Stempel and Westely 1981, 120). All researchers were instructed to approach each story in the same manner. "Quantitative analysis" is the application of numerical values to the rule-defined content. A computer program with the codes embedded was devised using *Microsoft Access*. This ensured that coders would not type incorrect numbers for the coding materials, but instead highlight the appropriate value on the computer screen. Finally, the "manifest content" is what was analyzed. In other words, coders were instructed to identify the text as written and code its surface meaning instead of trying to identify hidden or underlying messages.

The theory of content analysis as just outlined is quite straightforward; in practice, many checks must be put in place to ensure rigorous attention to detail. Moreover, when dealing with complex public policy issues, the personal opinion of the coder may make it difficult for some researchers to apply the coding rules consistently. To ensure the highest standards of coder reliability, the following checks were put in place. First, four coders were hired. These coders were all bilingual, so that they could analyze both the French and English news articles. Second, the coders each had different political leanings. On self-description, one coder was positioned on the left; one was moderate; one was to the right of centre; and one was "classically conservative," which to that coder meant that any change in public policy should, if possible, be avoided. There were two men and two women. In addition, the coders had differing educational backgrounds and geographical locations for their education. One was a recent psychology graduate from the University of British Columbia. The others were a second-year University of Toronto law student, a third-year political science major from University of Victoria, and a first-year McMaster graduate student who had just graduated from the University of Calgary's political science department.

Because of the diversity of opinions, educational backgrounds, and interests, we are confident that, when these coders came to agreement on what was written in the text or said in the television newscasts, it was an accurate appraisal. More important, we are confident that any four researchers following the same rules would produce similar results. In addition to periodic intercoder reliability tests, described below, all stories were examined twice. Every story was re-examined by a coder who had a different political perspective than the original coder. This not only ensured consistency between researchers, but it also resolved oversights and small judgment errors or discrepancies.

We conducted coder reliability tests throughout the duration of the content analysis. These tests were used to assess the clarity of the coding instrument, to train coders, and measure coder consistency. A conservative formula, which considers the element of chance, was used:

$$P_I = \frac{P_o - P_e}{1 - P_e}$$

P_I is the percentage of intercoder reliability; P_o is the percentage of observed agreement; and P_e is the percentage of agreement expected by chance (Stempel and Westley 1981, 143). These tests produced results with values that are conventionally considered well within acceptable limits. The intercoder score for the economic indicator study, for example, was high at 81.6 percent. This indicates that the categories developed to measure economic indicators actually did that. As noted above, when there were discrepancies in coding by different coders, they were reconciled by recourse to the decision rules and agreement of the individuals concerned. For these reasons we are confident in the results of the content analysis.

Sample

This study analyzed coverage of economic, social, and national unity issues by three television networks and three newspapers. From television we selected the national newscasts of the Canadian Broadcasting Corporation's flagship news program, *The National* and *The National Magazine*. We also selected the private broadcaster's national newscast, the *CTV News*. From the francophone media we selected Radio-Canada's *Le Téléjournal* and *Le Point*. Newspapers selected were the *Calgary Herald,* the *Globe and Mail*, and the Quebec daily *Le Devoir*. The *Calgary Herald* is part of the Southam chain of newspapers and underwent significant editorial-board changes when Hollinger Incorporated obtained controlling interest of Southam. It is regarded as one of the most profitable newspapers in the Southam chain. It also represents a western Canadian perspective. The *Globe and Mail,* at the time flagship of the Thomson chain, represents the "national paper of record" as well as a newspaper with a central-Canadian focus. *Le Devoir,* although not the highest-readership newspaper in Quebec, is the élite daily in the province. Although this is far from an exhaustive list of the newspapers and television programs in the country, it represents the major ownership chains as well as mixing private and public news outlets along with representation from different regions and both French- and English-language media.

Stories were selected using computerized databases of the transcripts of television broadcasts and the newsprint of newspapers. *Globe and Mail* stories were accessed by using Infoglobe, the online text search tool. The *Calgary Herald* was obtained through its in-house library search service. *Le Devoir* news was retrieved by CD-Rom from Micromedia. The English-language television transcripts were obtained from the National Media Archive. The French-language television transcripts were obtained from taping the newscasts of *Le Téléjournal* for one year. *Le Téléjournal* transcripts are the least reliable with respect to completeness of the holdings. No one in Canada consistently tapes or transcribes these newscasts. As a consequence, *Le Téléjournal* had to be recorded from cable in Calgary. Often the news was pre-empted by sporting events such as hockey games, the Olympics, and so on. As a result, if the program was delayed, it would not have been included in our sample because we recorded newscasts by preset times on a VCR. All attempts to find alternative tapes or transcripts through either Radio-Canada or private providers failed. The transcripts of the *Téléjournal* are therefore incomplete but are the best that were available.

Sample Issues

Considering the plethora of information in newspapers and on television on various public policy issues, we had to narrow our inquiry to a usable sample. For the economic issues, we chose to examine unemployment, employment, and inflation, using those terms as keywords along with the "Consumer Price Index" and "CPI" to find stories dealing with those topics. For social policy, we chose to narrow our examination to Supreme Court decisions. Previous research in this area has shown that the media tend to focus their examination on the Supreme Court decisions to when those decisions affect social policy. These issues tend to be contentious and provide an assessment of what news personnel consider newsworthy with respect to social change. The search term for social policy was "supreme court."

For national unity issues, again the task was to narrow rather than expand our focus of inquiry. An abundance of news on national unity is available to Canadians. One contentious issue area probed in the survey is the possibility of the partition of Quebec if the province were to secede after a "yes" vote in a referendum. In addition, the period during which we examined news coverage coincided with poll data on Canadian attitudes toward this issue. The search terms for this analysis were "Quebec and partition" or "separation." All stories captured under these search terms were analyzed from 1 July 1996 to 30 June 1997. A more detailed discussion of the variables and coding procedures is found in Appendix B.

The following three chapters provide the detailed results of the three content analyses and compare the coverage of public policy issues to that of journalists' own beliefs in those areas. We start with unemployment issues, where we find a close correlation between what journalists think about economic issues and their reporting of unemployment. We then turn to the coverage of Quebec partition. Finally we examine coverage of the Supreme Court and social issues and the relationship to journalists' opinions.

PART 3

ISSUES

CHAPTER 6

ECONOMIC ISSUES

This chapter summarizes the results of the content analysis of 116 *Globe and Mail,* 192 *Calgary Herald,* 152 *Le Devoir,* 37 *CTV News,* 49 CBC *National,* and 6 *National Magazine,* and 40 *Le Téléjournal* and *Le Point* stories from 1 July 1996 to 30 June 1997, for a total of 592 stories dealing with economic issues. All stories appearing in each news outlet for the specified period were coded. Consequently, the observed sample represents a total population rather than a random or constructed sample.

OVERVIEW OF COVERAGE

The *Globe and Mail* had the highest number of economic stories on inflation, unemployment, and employment. This is not surprising since the *Globe and Mail* takes pride in its business section and its overall coverage of corporate Canada. The Southam-owned *Calgary Herald* had the second-highest number of stories on economic topics. Following close behind was the Quebec daily, *Le Devoir.* Television coverage proved to be considerably less than that of newspapers on these issues. Considering that television is in some respects an abbreviated newspaper and statistical data do not make for engaging TV, lower coverage of economic questions is to be expected. *The National* was the television program most attentive to economic issues,

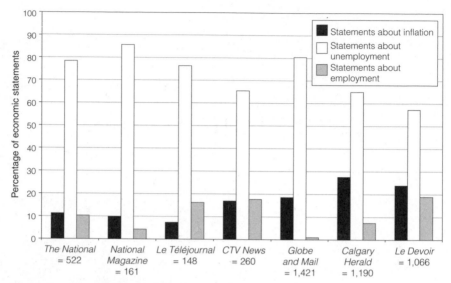

Figure 6.1   Attention to inflation, unemployment, and employment
NOTE: n = statements

followed by the *CTV News, The National Magazine,* and *Le Téléjournal.* As was mentioned in Chapter 5, *Le Téléjournal* figures may be under-represented because of incomplete sample collection.

For each news outlet, unemployment was the major focus of the economic stories we examined. Almost three-quarters (70.4 percent) of all news outlet attention focused on unemployment figures. This ranged from 57 percent of *Le Devoir's* attention to the three economic issues examined to a high of 86 percent of *The National Magazine's* (Figure 6.1).

During the sample period, inflation was the second most frequently discussed variable in most news outlets. The only exception was *Le Téléjournal,* where inflation was reported half as often as employment. Twenty percent of the combined economic coverage of newspapers and television programs examined inflation. Of the remainder, 9 percent reported on employment. Because so little attention is paid to inflation and employment, we will not be discussing those findings in detail. Instead, we focus on the monthly differences in attention to the unemployment rate. The attitudes and values of statements on unemployment and inflation are included in our discussion of ideology.

UNEMPLOYMENT

Regional Coverage

Nearly two-thirds (64 percent) of media attention directed to the unemployment rate dealt with national figures. National television news had the highest proportion of national unemployment statistics, which made up some 94 percent of CBC's and 87 percent of CTV's attention to unemployment in the year examined. *Le Téléjournal* had the least national coverage, comprising just under half of its total attention to unemployment (49 percent). *Le Devoir* paid more attention to the national unemployment rate (58 percent of its total unemployment coverage) than did French television. Of the English dailies examined, the *Calgary Herald* devoted 63 percent of its unemployment coverage to the national figures; the *Globe and Mail,* 52 percent.

The greatest amount of regional coverage was spent on Quebec. While it is not surprising that Quebec media focus on that province, we did not expect Quebec to be the focus of so much attention on *CTV News* or the *Globe and Mail.* Figure 6.2 isolates the attention paid to unemployment rates

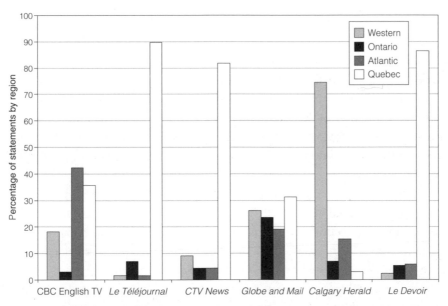

Figure 6.2   Media attention to seasonally adjusted regional unemployment rates, July 1996-June 1997

in the regions during 1996-7. Western provinces (British Columbia and the Prairies) received 31 percent of media attention; Ontario received 14 percent; and the Atlantic region received 15 percent of the attention. In contrast, Quebec obtained the lion's share, some 40 percent, of the total regional coverage.

Within the news agencies, *Le Téléjournal, CTV News,* and *Le Devoir* gave Quebec more than 85 percent of the regional unemployment coverage. The *Globe and Mail* gave it the most attention of any region, although Quebec still constituted only 31 percent of regional coverage. In fact, the *Globe and Mail* dispersed its regional coverage the most evenly between the provinces, with Western Canada receiving 26 percent, Ontario 24 percent, and Atlantic Canada 19 percent of the attention. CBC's *The National* and *The National Magazine* differ significantly from all other news organizations, with 42 percent of its coverage emphasizing the Atlantic Region. Not surprisingly, the *Calgary Herald* gave the Quebec unemployment figures the least attention – only 3 percent of its regional coverage. The bulk of the *Calgary Herald* attention focused on the western provinces at 75 percent. Since the unemployment rate differed significantly among regions, we will examine each region separately to see the type of attention paid by the media.

National Coverage
Unemployment statistics report on the previous month's figure. In order to determine whether the media accurately and consistently describe the Statistics Canada figures, we need to chart the unemployment rates from the previous month. Accordingly, the study examined media attention from July 1996 to June 1997, but we used the unemployment statistics from June 1996 to May 1997.

From June 1996 to May 1997 the national seasonally adjusted unemployment rate fluctuated between 9.3 and 10.0 percent. Within the twelve-month period the rate went down seven times, rose four times, and remained unchanged once. To examine the extent to which the media reflected these rate changes, we examined only statements that mention changes in the national unemployment rate. As can be seen in Figure 6.3, all media outlets, with the exception of *Le Téléjournal* and the *Calgary Herald,* overemphasized the increases in the unemployment rate and underemphasized the decreases in the national rate. During the instances when the unemployment rate was

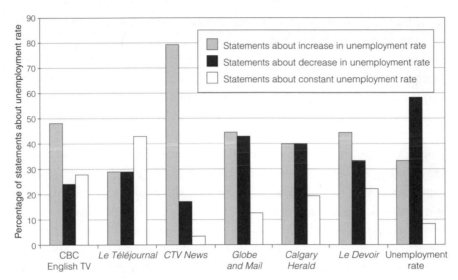

Figure 6.3 Seasonally adjusted national unemployment rate compared with media attention, July 1996–June 1997

on the increase (33 percent of the time in the 1996-7 period), newspapers and television generally gave those increases much more attention than they gave to decreases or to occasions when the rate did not change from month to month. CTV was most likely to emphasize the increases. In contrast, *Le Téléjournal* gave the bulk of its attention to the national rate to instances when the rate did not fluctuate. Of the remaining news outlets, increases in the national rate comprise an average of 44 percent: Figure 6.3 shows the specific rates ranging from 48 percent at English CBC to a comparative low of 40 percent at the *Calgary Herald*.

Just as the increases in the unemployment rate were overemphasized, decreases often went under-reported. During the 58 percent of the time that the rate declined, the average media attention to those declines was only 31 percent. The *Globe and Mail* gave the decreases the most attention, at 43 percent. *CTV News* provided the least attention to decreases in the national unemployment rate.

It has been well documented that the institutional bias of journalists is toward bad news. For example, David Harrington (1989) found over a twelve-year period that the American networks gave greater coverage to bad economic news. Similarly, former journalist Burton Pines found that American network television presented a distorted picture of the US economy: "Morning after morning, night after night, and one newsmagazine segment after another, viewers of network TV saw and heard a distorted picture of how their economy functioned and those who made it function. The American economy, they learned, was a tale of catastrophes, bankruptcies, fraud, and ineptness, which was dominated by white businessmen (and a few businesswomen) who were criminals and con men and by consumers who were stupid, gullible, and powerless. The tale was a litany of problems for which, inevitably, government was the preferred solution" (Pines 1994, 291). Likewise, Ted Smith (1988, 59) noted, "In general, the better the performance of the economy, the less coverage it received on network television."[1]

Clearly, greater emphasis on increasing unemployment at the expense of reporting declines in the jobless rate would illustrate this propensity. However, the mere reporting of the unemployment statistics only reveals what journalists consider newsworthy; it does not show the type of attention they provide to those rate changes. To examine the direction of coverage, statements were categorized by three values: neutral, positive, and negative. Considering that the unemployment rate declined more often than it rose during the period we analyzed, one would expect that the coverage would be supportive of the employment gains made in the country. To test this assumption we first examined the overall neutral, positive, and negative evaluations of the unemployment rate found in the television reports and dailies. The preponderance of coverage discusses the unemployment rate in a neutral, factual manner. Slightly less than three-quarters (73 percent) of the overall attention to unemployment is neutral. These comments tend to consist of repeating statistical figures. For example, on 8 November 1996, CBC's Alison Smith on *The National* reported the figures in this way: "More Canadians were looking for work last month. The unemployment rate edged up a notch to 10 percent." The number of jobs in Canada had actually grown during the previous months, but so had the number of people who were looking for them; hence the increase.

Eighty percent of the *Calgary Herald*'s statements on unemployment were neutral. For example, on 12 October 1996 the *Calgary Herald* reported on the city's unemployment figures for the month: "Calgary's unemployment rate dropped slightly last month, moving against the national trend that's giving Finance Minister Paul Martin a political headache. Calgary's rate dropped to 6.9 per cent in September from 7.1 per cent in August. The rate is down one full percentage point from a year ago, according to statistics released Friday" (Alberts and Steinhart 1996, A3). *The National* and *The National Magazine* had the smallest number of neutral statements on unemployment, comprising 55 percent of total unemployment statements. *CTV News* was more likely than *The National* to provide neutral descriptions of unemployment (68 percent), and the *Globe and Mail* reported unemployment in a neutral manner 76 percent of the time.

Of the statements that provided evaluations about unemployment, negative comments outweighed positive comments by an eight-to-one margin. The news agency with the highest proportion of unfavourable attention to the unemployment figures was CBC English television, where statements were nine times as likely to be critical of the unemployment figures than laudatory. The least critical news agency was the *Globe and Mail,* where negative comments were only three times as likely as positive comments.

Considering the above finding, that the news media focus on months where the unemployment rate increased over months where it declined, it is not surprising to find attention is more likely to evoke negative comments than positive ones. However, when one analyzes the data to examine how each change in the unemployment rate was treated, a more complex picture emerges.

When the unemployment rate increased, one would have expected more negative than positive attention to the change. After all, people don't usually regard high unemployment as a good thing, and that is certainly what our analysis of unemployment statistics during 1996-7 shows. Neutral statements comprised 79 percent of the overall attention, with negative statements outweighing positive statements by a nine-to-one margin. In fact, there were only nine positive statements during the whole year in all the news sources examined when the unemployment rate increased.

When the unemployment rate went down, there was an increase in both neutral comments and favourable ones. Overall, when the rate declined, neutral statements constituted 85 percent of the agenda. Of the few statements that provide assessments of the rate, they were eight times as likely to evoke a positive as a negative response. There were some slight variations in the percentages between the news agencies, but all reported declines in the unemployment rate in generally the same way.

However, when there was no change in the unemployment rate from the previous month, there were fewer neutral comments and generally more criticism of a static situation. Two-thirds of the overall attention to unemployment reported no change in the rate. CBC's flagship news show provided the smallest proportion of neutral statements, comprising 47 percent of the attention. All of the statements on *Le Téléjournal* were neutral when the rate did not change from one month to another. About half of the statements on *CTV News* and in the *Calgary Herald* were neutral. Three-quarters (75 percent) of the *Globe's* and almost three-quarters (73 percent) of *Le Devoir's* coverage were neutral. Of the evaluations, negative comments outnumbered positive comments by a nine-to-one margin. In fact, only the *Globe and Mail* provided any positive comments when the national unemployment rate was static.

These data indicate that regardless of the news agency examined, when it comes to reporting the unemployment rate, journalists emphasize bad news. When the news was positive they underplayed the positive direction of the indicator by merely reporting the rate or providing a minor positive comment. To illustrate better how reports of unemployment had little to do with actual changes in the unemployment rate, we charted the changes to the national rate with the positive, negative, and neutral attention each news agency gave unemployment during the year analyzed.

Figure 6.4 shows the month-by-month attention CBC's *The National* and *The National Magazine* gave to the unemployment rate. In August 1996, the national unemployment rate went down from 9.9 to 9.5. This was the single largest decline in the unemployment rate since November 1994, yet the attention to the change reported in September was negligible. In every case where the unemployment rate substantially decreased compared with previous months, CBC ignored those improvements. CBC was more likely to be critical of unemployment statistics when there was little or no change.

For example, in March 1997 the network provided the most negative comments about unemployment for the entire year during a period when unemployment rate was undergoing slight declines and little change. Peter Mansbridge introduced the lead story on 7 March 1997 saying, "Good evening. It's like a giant boulder that nobody seems able to budge. Certainly not the million and a half Canadians who are looking for work. The unemployment rate last month was 9.7 percent. The same as the month before, and the month before that." In fact, the national unemployment rate was 9.8 percent during the previous month and the month before that it was 10.0. *The National Magazine* followed the lead of *The National* with two features during March on job creation. On 18 March 1997, the focus of *The National Magazine* was on the change from the industrial to the information age. Brian Stewart noted, "It is eerie. Our national wealth increases, yet all around, as in the '90s, lie the dusty abandoned factories, the heavy latent air of vanished workers. Economists say we're moving from the industrial age into something vague, almost ephemeral; the information era. Well, it's an era in which the casualties of competition are very high." Added to these generally negative stories was a 28 March 1997 *National Magazine* feature on youth unemployment.

The National and *The National Magazine* clearly emphasized the stagnant unemployment rate. They also misrepresented it, stating that the rate remained the same when in fact it declined. During April the unemployment rate declined again and the network news shows completely ignored the positive news: no mention at all was made of the drop in unemployment

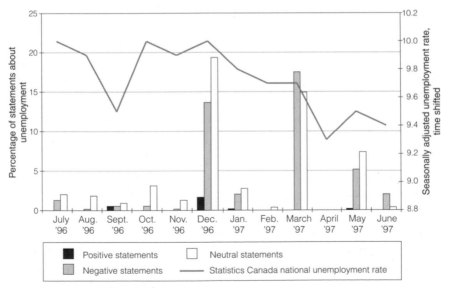

Figure 6.4   Attention to unemployment compared with seasonally adjusted rate, CBC English-language television, July 1996–June 1997

NOTE: n = 543 statements

from the previous month. Thomas Carlyle may have called economics the dismal science; CBC seems to think that the only economic news is dismal news.

CBC's French television network was less likely than the English CBC service to emphasize the national unemployment statistics. Instead, *Le Téléjournal* focused nearly as much attention (46 percent) on the Quebec unemployment rate as it did (48 percent) on the national rate. As a result, the attention *Le Téléjournal* allocated toward unemployment in the fall months of 1996 was more instructive of what was happening in Quebec than what was reflected in the national unemployment figures. The only time national figures dominated the news agenda on *Le Téléjournal* was in February and April of 1997. The negative attention in February focused more on the lack of change in the national unemployment rate than on anything happening in Quebec. When Jean-François Lépine questioned Finance Minister Paul Martin in a 17 February 1997 *Le Point* interview, the emphasis was on the apparent failure of the Liberal government to provide jobs: "Mr. Minister, the Liberals campaigned under the slogan 'Jobs, jobs, jobs.' The reality has been 'no jobs, no jobs, no jobs.'" In using this type of question, as well as by focusing on the stagnant unemployment rate, journalists claimed that the Liberal government failed in its 1993 election campaign promise to get Canadians working. One result of adopting such a short-term view was that few people were aware that since 1993 the unemployment rate had in fact declined by nearly 2 percentage points. In a rolling survey of Canadians polled during the 1997 election campaign, for example, "39 percent thought the unemployment rate had gone up since the Liberals had come to power, and only 19 percent perceived it to have gone down" (Blais et al. 1998, 13).

The public's perception of the economy underlines the power the media have in shaping our understanding of the world. One of the essential issues in the 1993 election campaign centred on the claim made by Kim Campbell that unemployment would remain in double digits until the turn of the century. The Liberal promise of "jobs, jobs, jobs" was the counterclaim that the Liberals would bring unemployment to a single-digit figure in their mandate. By that standard, the reduction of unemployment from 11.9 percent in 1993 to 9.7 in January 1997 showed a remarkable success on the part of the Liberal government. The decline in the unemployment rate during that period, however, was not treated as a success story by any news outlet we examined.

In April the negative commentary focused exclusively on the national figures. The best example of the propensity of news to emphasize the negative over other considerations can be seen in the CBC French television service. While CBC French-language services were particularly interested in the Quebec unemployment rate, that interest was overridden when bad economic news was reflected in the national rate. Figure 6.5 indicates not only that CBC French-language television emphasized the negative but also that its attention to the province or the country depended more on bad news than on any sense of nationalism. Inroads in the national unemployment rate were downplayed or ignored when the provincial rate was high. The same thing happened (not shown in the figure) when the provincial rate decreased, only then criticism or negative coverage was directed at the national rate.

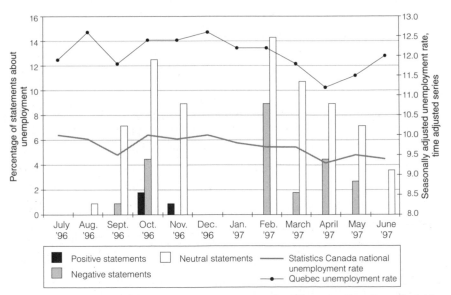

Figure 6.5 Attention to unemployment compared with seasonally adjusted rated, CBC French-language television, July 1996–June 1997

NOTE: n = 112 statements

The inclination to emphasize the negative, or in some cases to seek out the negative side of economic news, can also be seen in Figure 6.6, where we show CTV's attention to the unemployment rate. As was noted earlier, the national rate comprised 87 percent of CTV's unemployment focus. When the national unemployment rate had a slight decline from 10.0 to 9.9 percent between June and July of 1996, CTV's response was to focus on the poor performance in Quebec. Lloyd Robertson's introduction on 9 August 1996 portrayed a dismal scene: "The economic picture being painted out of Quebec today was anything but robust. Two straight months of whopping job losses have the economy there in a tailspin." Just as the public broadcaster ignored the unemployment rate when jobless figures were on the decline, so too did *CTV News*. In April, after the March figures showed unemployment was at eighteen-month low, there was scant attention paid to what looks like a good-news story. Instead, the focus switched to figures that indicated ongoing youth unemployment. For example, Roger Smith on the 18 April 1997 *CTV News* provided this commentary: "Last election, Chrétien promised lots of jobs. So just how much did he deliver? Campaigning Liberals will point to the bright side: 750,000 new jobs since they took power. Unemployment down from 11.2 percent to 9.2 percent. But look at the dark side: 1.4 million are still out of work. Youth unemployment is 16 percent. And the official numbers don't even count half a million so-called discouraged workers who simply stopped looking."

When the unemployment rate had a 0.4 percentage-point decline from the previous month, *CTV News* did not provide any positive commentary. In contrast, when the unemployment rate rose by half that amount, Lloyd Robertson described it as a "sharp increase." On the 9 May 1997 *CTV News*, he said, "Prime Minister Jean Chrétien was confronted forcefully today by the underlying agony facing 1.5 million Canadians. First thing this morning new figures came out showing a sharp increase in the unemployment rate." The most obvious explanation why an equal decline in the unemployment rate was not described in a similarly dramatic way is that negativity trumps all other news considerations.

Of all the news outlets examined, the *Globe and Mail* provided proportionately the least amount of negative commentary. While nine out of every ten assessments on television were negative, the *Globe and Mail* was likely only seven times out of ten to provide a negative spin to unemployment

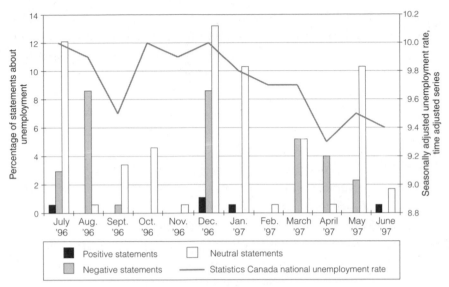

Figure 6.6   Attention to unemployment compared with seasonally adjusted rate, *CTV News,* July 1996–June 1997

NOTE: n = 174 statements

statistics. For the *Globe's* Bruce Little, the unemployment figures represented a situation where, even though the fundamentals favoured job growth, the country was still unable to achieve it: "Another month, another depressing set of job numbers. The unemployment rate remained stuck at 10 percent in November, reflecting an economy that is still having trouble creating new jobs for Canadians, even after 18 months of falling interest rates and despite solid economic growth in the third quarter" (*Globe and Mail,* 7 December 1996, B1). What differentiated the *Globe* from television news was that, despite the overall negative picture on unemployment, journalists such as Little were still able to bring forward some positive news on the jobless rates. Little noted, for example, that the meaning of the numbers depends on the region where they were compiled and then he showed how the western provinces were in fact faring in the employment picture: "How the job picture looks to Canadians depends on where they live, because the East-West divide in Canada's labour market is starker than ever. In the past 12 months, Quebec and the Atlantic Provinces have lost 27,000 jobs while Ontario and the four western provinces have gained 232,000."

The *Globe and Mail* had a preference similar to that of television. The newspaper emphasized the negative over the positive in the unemployment rates, but in May 1997, when the unemployment rate showed a consistent decline, it did provide some relief to the endless barrage of negativity (see Figure 6.7). Unlike the CBC networks and CTV, the *Globe and Mail* provided mostly neutral statements on unemployment, but, more important, it provided almost as many positive as negative comments about changes in unemployment statistics. This is unusual compared to the predominance of a negative spin to economic statistics among the media surveyed. Although some of the comments did come from self-serving politicians, the fact that the *Globe and Mail* reproduced these opinions contrasted with the information that television news presented. For example, on 10 May 1997 Robert Matas summarized the argument of the finance minister of British Columbia: "Earlier this year, the province's unemployment rate was lower, but few new jobs were being created. Statistically, it looked good; but in reality, people were not looking for work. The jobless rate is not a good indication of the health of the economy, he said. The real key is job creation. In the past

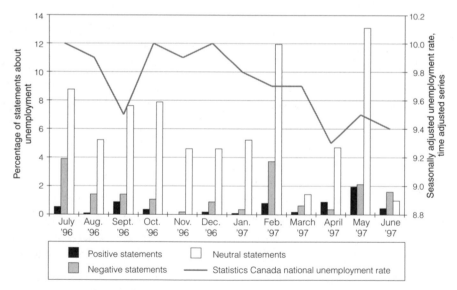

Figure 6.7   Attention to unemployment compared with seasonally adjusted rate, *Globe and Mail*, July 1996–June 1997

NOTE: n = 1,130 statements

month, more people were in the job market and more work was available. 'That's a good sign,' Mr. Petter said, 'I see that as indicating economic growth'" (Matas 1997, A8).

To be fair to television news, newspapers have significantly more room to qualify and explain the numbers they present, and as we have said, numbers make for boring television. The purpose of this study, however, is not to compare the relative strengths of newspapers and television, but to show that newsroom decisions on newsworthiness affect the way that economic stories are reported. Regardless of the news agency, there is a tendency to downplay positive economic news and focus on bleak economic pictures.

In contrast to television news, where a significant amount of attention was focused on the November unemployment figures, coverage in the *Calgary Herald* was highest in January (see Figure 6.8). As a result, it emphasized the decline in the unemployment figures and provided more positive than negative comment on the unemployment picture. In that month, for example, Jim Cunningham and Carol Howes reported, "Alberta's unemployment rate has dropped to 6.3 per cent – painting a job picture that hasn't looked so bright since the boom years of the late 1970s and early 1980s. 'The last time we saw figures like this was back in 1982,' Archie Clark, director of strategic planning and research for Advanced Education and Career Development, said Friday. 'The labor force in Alberta is performing differently and it's better and it's running contrary to everywhere else in the country'" (Cunningham and Howes 1997, A1).

Nonetheless, even the generally good news on unemployment in Calgary did not stop the *Calgary Herald* from providing three times as many negative as positive statements about unemployment. In January, six *Calgary Herald* stories provided positive comments on unemployment. In contrast, in February at a time when Statistics Canada reported a slight decline in the jobless rate, there were sixteen stories in the *Calgary Herald* that provided negative comments on unemployment. Despite the cheery statements from Cunningham and Howe in January, stories in February focused on the bleak national picture: "Few generations of Canadians have been forced to run the marathon of their youth before finding a decent job. However, a new study says the four million members of the Baby Bust generation, aged 15 to 24, face years of slogging in low-pay, low-skill 'McJobs' if they find work at all. 'Everyone's having a difficult time in the 1990s, but this group is having an

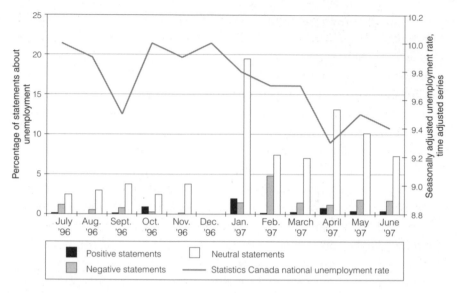

Figure 6.8 Attention to unemployment compared with seasonally adjusted rate,
Calgary Herald, July 1996-June 1997
NOTE: n = 615 statements

especially difficult time,' says author Gordon Betcherman, a research director for Canadian Research Policy Networks Inc." (*Calgary Herald,* 12 February 1997, A14).

Le *Devoir,* unlike the anglophone news outlets, might be expected to
emphasize the negative aspects of the unemployment rate. For the period
we analyzed, Quebec's unemployment rate was one of the highest in the
country. In contrast to Alberta's rate of 6.9 percent, Quebec's rate stayed in
the 12 percent range for most of the year, reaching a low of only 11.2 percent. The nine-to-one ratio of negative to positive stories in *Le Devoir* is at
least consistent with the overall gloomy economic picture of the province
(see Figure 6.9).

The networks and the daily papers alike emphasized increases over decreases in unemployment. In months when the unemployment rate went
down, there was scant attention to the national picture or the focus shifted
to a region where the unemployment rate was higher than the national
average. In addition, negative comments were made assessing changes in the
unemployment rate, with statements to the effect that the jobless figure was

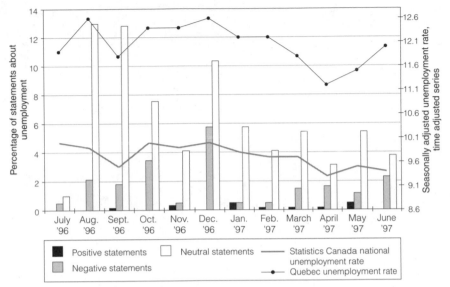

Figure 6.9   Attention to unemployment compared with seasonally adjusted rate,
Le Devoir, July 1996-June 1997
NOTE: n = 609 statements

either not going down fast enough or was too static for economic growth.
Figure 6.10 combines all the data to illustrate that, on aggregate, the months
with the most negative commentary were associated with the slight increases in the unemployment statistics.

To say that journalists mirror events that take place in society grossly
simplifies their role in presenting, producing, and packaging information.
This brief overview of unemployment reporting indicates not just that news
producers emphasize bad news over good news, which is expected, but that
they do so in several systematic ways. First, the news stressed statistics that
showed the economy performing poorly. Second, in the absence of poor
national figures, the news media typically highlighted regions or sectors,
such as youth, that at the time were being hit hard by unemployment. Third,
regions in the country that were sources of positive economic news were
ignored. More important, high-employment regions were not analyzed in
any depth so that their success in reducing unemployment might serve as
models for the rest of the country. At the same time as Canadians were being
told accurately enough about the poor economic prospects in Quebec, they

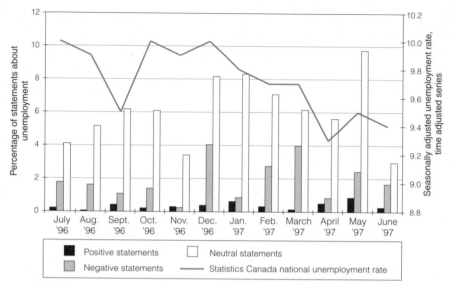

Figure 6.10   Aggregate of attention to unemployment compared with seasonally
adjusted rate, July 1996–June 1997
NOTE: n = 3,336 statements

were not being told about how Alberta had managed to reduce its unemployment rate to 63 percent of Quebec's. As a result, the fiscally conservative and economically successful policies in Alberta were ignored. In the
next section we see how the media accounted for, or explained away, the
hapless policies pursued by such high-unemployment provinces as Quebec.

Causes of Unemployment and Solutions to It

The preceding analysis illustrates the tendency for Canadian journalists to
emphasize negative economic news and under-report positive news, but it
does not provide an assessment of the kinds of policy statements that were
presented to account for unemployment. In addition to reporting when
unemployment went up, stayed the same, or declined, and to indicating
whether those statistics boded well or ill for the country, we also captured
assessments of what sources and journalists presented as the causes of unemployment and the ways to reduce it. The latter two types of analytical
statements appear less frequently than simple presentations of information
that effectively interprets itself. That is, because high unemployment is self-

evidently bad economic news, the balance between good- and bad-news stories regarding the employment rate is inherently significant. By providing an additional assessment of what the good or bad news meant, additional information was provided.

As can be seen in Figure 6.11, the bulk of attention to unemployment, as expected, simply provided information on the direction of the indicator. In our sample, 76 percent of CBC English (i.e., TV's *The National* and *The National Magazine*), 80 percent of CBC French (i.e., Radio-Canada's *Le Téléjournal* and *Le Point* TV programs), 81 percent of *CTV News*, 82 percent of the *Globe and Mail*, 84 percent of the *Calgary Herald*, and 79 percent of *Le Devoir's* coverage focused on changes in the indicator. CBC English, *CTV News*, and the *Globe and Mail* paid more attention to the causes of unemployment than to its solutions. By "causes of unemployment" we referred to stories explaining why the unemployment rate was so high; "solutions" were accounts of how to reduce it. For Radio-Canada and *Le Devoir*, more attention was paid to solutions than to causes of unemployment. The *Calgary Herald* gave about the same attention to causes of unemployment as to solutions.

To simplify reporting of the results, we created an index of economic opinion on the causes and solutions to unemployment. Similar to the index

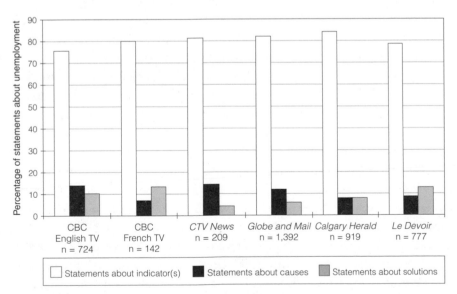

Figure 6.11   Overall attention to unemployment, July 1996-June 1997

on economic beliefs developed in the survey, all statements that identified a cause or solution were recoded into a three-point scale representing "right," "neutral," and "left." The higher the score, the more the statement provided a "left" response. The recoding was straightforward: statements advocating greater government intervention in the economy as a solution to unemployment, or the reduction of government intervention in the economy as the cause of unemployment, were coded as "left." Conversely, calls for tax cuts as a means to increase employment as a solution or of heavy government regulation as a cause of it were coded as "right." Neutral statements included those that simply provided information or did not advocate either free market or government intervention.

There are dramatic differences in the way the various news outlets provided opinions and attitudes on the causes of unemployment. As shown in Figure 6.12, CBC television was the most likely of any news organization to provide more left rather than right opinions on unemployment. More than half the time (53 percent), when the CBC English sample mentioned the causes of unemployment, they argued that the government was not doing enough for the unemployed. For example, on the unemployment feature on the 23 December 1996 *National Magazine,* host Hana Gartner asked her guest, "Harold, are people correct in making connections between deficit and unemployment?" To this Harold Chorney, an economist from Concordia University, replied, "Sure, I mean many economists would admit, even those who tend to be quite conservative, that if you cut back deficits, you're going to slow down economic growth. And the unemployment rate will rise. So a lot of the stagnation on our employment markets is directly related to the decision of the federal and provincial governments to reduce their debt-loads and to crunch their deficits." Despite Chorney's claim, conservative economists do not typically hold this view.

No other news agency we examined consistently emphasizes the left-of-centre position to the extent that English-language CBC does. Even the French-language CBC service was more likely to present the conservative opinion on unemployment in half of the statements, with the left-wing position comprising only 20 percent. In contrast, CTV provided just slightly more right- than left-of-centre views on unemployment, with the plurality of opinion being neutral. English-language newspapers were more likely to present the right-wing perspective on the causes of unemployment, with

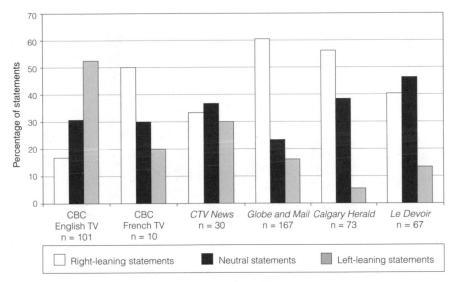

Figure 6.12   Statements about causes of unemployment, July 1996-June 1997

61 percent of the *Globe and Mail* and 56 percent of the *Calgary Herald* presenting the views of those who champion debt reduction and lower taxation. An example of such opinion was represented in a *Globe and Mail* Focus story (26 October 1996, D1) by Greg Ip, who stated, "Quebec's tax and debt burdens are already the country's second highest (after Newfoundland), while the province relies on relatively less corporate income taxes but more on payroll and capital taxes than the others in the interest of revenue stability. This has turned the tax system into a killer of jobs and investment." Even though most of the opinion in *Le Devoir* favoured a neutral stance, 40 percent of the coverage emphasized right-wing explanations for the causes of unemployment, compared with only 13 percent offering left-wing arguments.

At first blush, the solutions to unemployment seem to contradict or balance the opinions expressed on the causes of unemployment. As can be seen in Figure 6.13, CBC English provided predominately (51 percent) neutral statements on the solutions to unemployment and presented arguments on the left only slightly more often than those on the right (28 percent left versus 21 percent right). In contrast, CBC French had 42 percent of its coverage on the left compared with 26 percent on the right, nearly the exact reverse of its coverage on the causes of unemployment. *CTV News* also

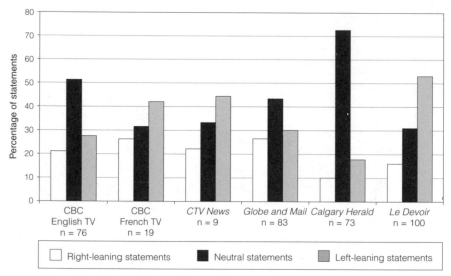

Figure 6.13   Statements about solutions to unemployment, July 1996–June 1997

provided proportionately more statements on the left than on the right, whereas on the causes of unemployment it seemed to present a balanced picture. Coverage of solutions to unemployment in the *Globe and Mail* was also different from the causes presented. The *Globe and Mail,* which provided a predominately right-of-centre perspective of the causes of unemployment, presented slightly more left (30 percent) versus right (27 percent) statements on the solutions to unemployment. The overwhelming right-of-centre coverage in the *Calgary Herald* on the causes of unemployment became primarily a neutral stance on the solutions to unemployment (73 percent), with the balance providing slightly more left rather than right statements. Coverage in *Le Devoir* also seemed to be divided, with 53 percent of the coverage on the left for solutions compared with only 13 percent on the left for causes.

The proportion of attention to solutions on the left compared with those on the right tends to obscure the overall trend in coverage and masks the true nature of media attention to unemployment. As is noted in Figure 6.13, the number of stories dealing with solutions is quite small in some news outlets and such stories tend to be proportionately fewer than the number of stories on the causes of unemployment, as is indicated in Figure 6.12. In order to grasp the complete picture of coverage of the unemployment story, the solutions index was combined with the causes index to indicate the overall trend of coverage. Those results are presented in Figure 6.14. The number of comments on causes of unemployment outweighed the number of comments on solutions, as the preceding figures show. In Figure 6.14 we see as well that English-language CBC remained the news outlet with the highest proportion of comments on the left, at 43 percent. Despite Radio-Canada's scoring 42 percent on the left, it was more balanced than English-language CBC because it also had 30 percent of its comments on the right, whereas only 18 percent of the CBC-English comments were on the right. Radio-Canada thus provided more balanced coverage overall than did its English-language counterpart.

In contrast, CTV's coverage was almost balanced, with 36 percent favouring a neutral position and 33 percent on the left, with the balance, 31 percent, on the right. The *Globe and Mail* and the *Calgary Herald* both had more overall coverage on the right than on the left. For the *Globe and Mail,* 45 percent of the statements were on the right, with 28 percent neutral and 27 percent on the left. One might describe the *Globe and Mail* as being just as far to the right as the English-language CBC was to the left. Indeed, the *Globe* has

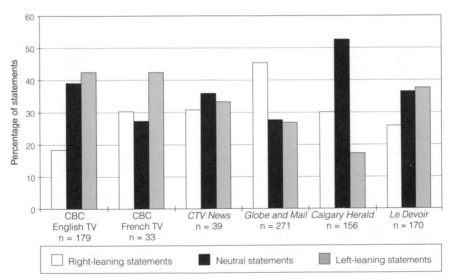

Figure 6.14   Index of causes of and solutions to unemployment, July 1996–June 1997

45 percent of statements on the right compared with 43 percent of CBC-English's on the left. It should be noted, however, that the *Globe and Mail* is relatively more balanced than English-language CBC, simply because it also provides 27 percent of its coverage on the left compared, as noted above, with 18 percent of English-language CBC coverage on the right. Similarly, for the *Calgary Herald,* 30 percent of the combined causes and solutions statements were on the right, compared with 17 percent on the left. However, what distinguished the *Calgary Herald* from the rest of the media outlets was the relatively high number of neutral statements, some 53 percent of the causes and solution index. For *Le Devoir,* comments on the left were more numerous than those on the right, comprising 38 percent of the attention, compared with 26 percent on the right.

Inflation

A total of 27 statements, from the CBC English-language service, from the *Globe and Mail,* the *Calgary Herald,* and *Le Devoir,* were made on inflation and the economy. The media consensus was that inflation is needed to stimulate the economy. This apparent unanimity seems to be the result of a controversial and widely publicized paper by University of Québec economist Pierre Fortin. In fact, most of the stories on this relationship referred to Fortin in some manner. Only Terence Corcoran in the 15 November 1996 *Globe and Mail* (B2) questioned the soundness of Fortin's proposal: "There are, however, still many obstacles to a full-employment labour market. No matter how much the Bank of Canada tried to boost the economy with inflation – even if Canadians could be fooled by the illusion of easy money – it could not overcome the unemployment built into the economy over the past three decades of government intervention. To really get unemployment down, much more work is needed to root out the real causes."

This view was clearly in the minority. Another notable *Globe and Mail* editorial writer came to a different conclusion. William Thorsell argued in favour of modest inflation: "Zero inflation requires many workers to accept literal wage reductions, as the relative prices of labour change in a dynamic market. In practice, this is very hard to achieve, so zero inflation actually clogs up the price mechanism for the critical factor of labour." He continued to explain: "As I have argued in this space for several years, low stable inflation – about 3 per cent – is necessary to lubricate the price system, to avoid irrational imbalances in the nominal value of assets and debts, and to reduce the terrible risks of general deflation. The Bank of Canada and the Chrétien government should eat some crow and raise the current target range for inflation, aiming for 3 per cent, in the interest of the unemployed, the poor and, therefore, the rest of us" (Thorsell 1996, D6).

The idea of inflation helping the economy crept into other stories as well. In *Le Devoir,* the Quebec deputy finance minister was quoted disparaging the economic policies of the federal government. Among his complaints, he argued that inflation could be used to help unemployment: "He accuses Mr. Martin of having lowered his sights and having not shown any imagination. 'Month after month, the situation, far from improving, gets worse. And, in that time, it is necessary to test everything,' the deputy [minister] charged. He believes that several avenues could have been explored, such as the reduction of Employment Insurance contributions, in order to encourage the Finance Minister to lower corporate taxes in order to recover significant sums that could have been reinvested in job creation. The Bank of Canada could also, he suggests, increase the rate of inflation to stimulate employment" (Richer 1996).

What is remarkable about the coverage of this question is not the content of the debate on whether it is sound economics to argue that modest inflationary pressures would stimulate the economy, but that there was so little debate on this issue at all.

Economic Wisdom

The reports on unemployment, employment, and inflation reveal a startling similarity between journalists' beliefs about the relationship between inflation and unemployment and their reporting practices. It is rare in social science research to have a perfect relationship, but the opinions journalists hold concerning the connection between unemployment and inflation almost identically mirror how they report the issue.

It should be recalled that the journalists were asked a question on their thoughts about the relationship between unemployment and inflation. The question asked: "It is sometimes said that when Canada's economy has low inflation and prices don't change much, there is high unemployment. Do you think this statement is completely true; largely true; somewhat true; not really true; or not at all true?" Only 10 percent of the journalists think that it is "not at all true." Half of the English and French journalists think that the statement is "somewhat true." When we examine the data of news coverage we find that, when journalists report on inflation and its relationship to unemployment, they overwhelmingly report that low inflation causes unemployment. All of CBC English-language, 73 percent of the *Globe and Mail*, 79 percent of the *Herald*, and 90 percent of *Le Devoir*'s coverage on this question argued that way.

IDEOLOGICAL CONGRUENCE

So far we have shown that, on the question of unemployment, journalists focus on the bad news. This observation, combined with the finding that little overall attention is placed on rising employment statistics, invariably presents a gloomy picture of the economy. But do these findings reflect journalists' personal opinions or just an occupational bias toward bad news? When they reported causes and solutions to unemployment, CBC English-language journalists, for example, tended to present left-wing more often than right-wing opinions. How do these findings reflect the opinions held by journalists? Is there a way to test the degree to which a journalist holds an opinion on the economy and how he or she reports economic issues?

To make such a comparison we draw upon the economic index reported in Chapter 4. The mean score of CBC English-language journalists is 2.2750 on the three-point economic conservative index, which places their views on capitalism and the economy at the left-of-centre position. The mean score for private-sector journalists is 2.0156, which places them at a centre position on economic issues. If the theory that journalists will promote ideas closest to their own is correct, we should expect to find that an index of causes and solutions in the news coverage of the economy closely mirrors the index positions indicated in the survey.

To test this expectation we recoded the causes and solutions of unemployment, employment, and inflation to correspond to a three-point economic index. We then recoded *CTV News,* the *Calgary Herald,* and the *Globe and Mail* to represent English-speaking news media. CBC English-language television represents CBC on this issue. The same process was done for the francophone media. The hypothesis being tested, therefore, is that the ideology of journalists is reflected in their news stories.

H_1: CBC English-language news stories will provide proportionately more statements arguing a government intervention position on unemployment than a free market position.

H_2: Private-sector news reports will provide a balance of information on unemployment.

H_3: French media reports will provide a balance of information on unemployment.

The first hypothesis is accepted. The mean score of CBC English-language journalists is 2.2750, while the combined index of causes and solutions gives a mean score of 2.2316. Comparing CBC with all other English-language news stories provides a t-test value of 6.915 and a two-tailed significance of $p > 0.001$. In ordinary common-sense language, statements presented on CBC television news that described the causes or gave solutions to unemployment favoured a government intervention approach. Such a numerical value indicates the opinion presented over English-language CBC was significantly different from both private English-language news outlets and from the neutral position.

The second hypothesis is also accepted. Anglophone private-sector journalists have a mean score of 2.0156, which represents a centre position on economic issues. The mean score represented by the statements made in the *Calgary Herald,* the *Globe and Mail,* and in the *CTV News* is 1.9853 with a t-test value of 4.173 at the two-tailed significance level of $p > 0.001$ compared with English-language CBC. This means that the coverage of unemployment was statistically different from that of CBC. It also shows that the private English-language news was closer to a neutral and balanced approach to economic reporting than was the CBC's English service. This does not mean that right- or left-wing opinions on the economic issues we examined were not discussed, but that they were balanced against each other and that neutral statements were also reported.

Hypothesis 3 is also accepted. The French news agencies provide a clear answer to the question of journalist opinion being mirrored in news content. The mean score reported in Chapter 4 for French-speaking journalists is 2.0394. In the survey, there were no statistical differences between the private- and public-sector journalists on this issue. The content analysis of French-language CBC provided a mean score of 2.1358, while *Le Devoir* produces a mean score of 2.0342. The independent *t*-test revealed no statistically significant differences between the two groups. Just as in the survey, Quebec news stories presented on average a moderate or balanced view on unemployment.

SUMMARY AND DISCUSSION

Let us summarize the findings of this chapter:

1   Of the news outlets examined, the *Globe and Mail* paid the most attention to unemployment, employment, and inflation. Radio-Canada (*Le Téléjournal* and *Le Point*) paid the least amount of attention to these economic indicators. In general, television paid less attention to these issues than did newspapers.

2   At 70 percent, most discussions of economic indicators were focused on unemployment. Nearly two-thirds (64 percent) of the attention to unemployment rates discussed the national figures. Of the regions, the most amount of coverage was focused on Quebec, a chronically high-unemployment province.

3   News agencies predominately discussed the unemployment rate in a neutral, factual manner. Slightly less than three-quarters (73 percent) of the overall attention to unemployment was neutral. These comments tended to report statistical figures. Of the statements that provided evaluations about unemployment, negative comments outweighed positive comments by an eight-to-one margin.

4   Media coverage also paid more attention to instances when the unemployment rate increased than to when it decreased. In the months when the unemployment rate declined there was scant attention to it or the focus shifted to a region or sector where the unemployment rate was higher than the national average.

5   For the entire year, there were only 27 statements in total from CBC English-language service, the *Globe and Mail,* the *Calgary Herald,* and *Le*

Devoir on the role of inflation and the economy. The consensus is that inflation was needed to stimulate the economy.

6 Reports on unemployment, employment, and inflation reveal a remarkable similarity between journalists' personal views of the relationship between inflation and unemployment and their reporting practices. The survey of journalists' opinions indicated that they believe there is a trade-off between employment and inflation. The news coverage overwhelmingly reports that low inflation causes unemployment.

7 To test whether personal opinions of journalists influenced the way they reported the news, an index of journalist opinion was compared with an index of news coverage. Three hypotheses were developed and tested. All three were accepted.

This chapter reveals that on economic issues the personal views of journalists were closely reflected in the stories they presented. In the survey we found that, for the most part, English- and French-speaking journalists tended to have a moderate or middle-of-the-road view on economic issues. They supported capitalism and free markets, but at the same time were receptive to the goals, if not the outcomes, of communism. When we compared their general economic views with how selected television and newspapers reported on the unemployment rate, employment, and inflation, we also saw a middle-of-the-road picture. News coverage on *CTV News* provided a balanced perspective on the causes and solutions to unemployment. In some instances, government-based solutions were suggested as a way to improve the economy, and at other times there were calls for the loosening of regulation or for tax cuts. In all, the approach tended to balance these opinions and closely reflects the fact that journalists themselves see both sides of the economic argument as having merit enough to be presented to the public. The *Globe and Mail* and the *Calgary Herald* each offered more statements on the right than on the left. As we recall from Chapter 4, private-sector journalists were stronger in their views on the desirability of free markets and capitalism than were public-sector journalists.

The opinions of CBC journalists were also remarkably consistent with how they reported on the economy. In the survey, the opinions of CBC English-language journalists were left of centre. These journalists were less

likely than private-sector journalists or French-speaking journalists to see
the benefits of capitalism and were more likely to support government solutions to public policy problems. These views were reflected in English-
language CBC stories on the economy. Coverage on English-language CBC
was more critical of government cutbacks and less likely to advocate tax cuts
as a means to boost economic performance.

There were other considerations that influenced the construction of the
news agenda. Most news outlets emphasized negative news over positive
news on the economy. Regions and sectors with poor economic performance were highlighted more frequently than regions or sectors with good
economic performance. The news outlet with the most emphasis on bad
news was the English-language CBC. The *Globe and Mail* was the least likely
to introduce a negative spin when unemployment figures were in decline.

This chapter also shows that ownership has little to do with coverage of
economic news. There were no statistical differences between the differently
owned private news outlets. The Baton-owned *CTV News,* then Thomson-
owned *Globe and Mail,* and the Southam-controlled *Calgary Herald* did not
have any statistically significant differences in their ideological profile. Indeed, there were no differences between the two francophone news outlets
or between French- and English-language news. The only news organization that was statistically different from the rest was the CBC. We conclude,
therefore, that public or private ownership of the media outlet does influence the coverage of economic issues. Ironically, it is the private sector that
provides the balanced approach to economic news reporting. Despite the
CBC's mandate to provide balance, it was more likely to present a left-of-
centre perspective of the economy.

These results should not come as a surprise. In the survey, we did find that
private- and public-sector journalists are different from each other in their
values regarding economic issues. What this clearly demonstrates is that journalists do not provide balanced or objective reporting on the economy. Journalists in CBC were more likely to select sources that confirmed their personal
views on the economy. Private-sector journalists did so as well, but they
provided more sources that disagreed with their own views, thus offering
balanced coverage to their audiences. In the next chapter we examine whether
the same holds true for national unity. While postmaterialism does hold an

economic perspective, it also has a dimension on regime threat. We now test whether journalist opinions on national unity translate to news coverage and direction on those issues. In other words, is the coverage of national unity correlated to what journalists thought about the issue?

CHAPTER 7

PARTITION OF QUEBEC

The lords of our national media, with a few exceptions, such as CTV and some factions in *The Globe and Mail,* have been exposed, in Rooseveltian terms, as "pious frauds." Their only concern for media concentration is to preserve it for themselves. Their principal concern in constitutional matters is to retain their own influence on the discussion, no matter how discredited their policy in the eyes of the majority of Canadians (Conrad Black, annual shareholders meeting of Hollinger Incorporated, 28 May 1997).

This chapter summarizes the results of the content analysis of 5 *National,* 10 *Le Téléjournal,* 2 *CTV News,* 15 *Globe and Mail,* 25 *Calgary Herald,* and 9 *Le Devoir* stories from 1 July 1996 to 30 June 1997, for a total of 66 stories on the proposed partition of Quebec being a plausible consequence of a positive outcome of a referendum vote on Quebec sovereignty. All the stories that appeared in these news outlets for the period we covered were coded. Again, therefore, the observed sample represents a total population rather than a random or constructed sample. Several tests of coder reliability were conducted throughout the procedure. The results of these tests indicate an acceptable percentage of coder agreement. The intercoder reliability score for the partition of Quebec study was 0.81. As in other content analyses, the unit of analysis was the statement. To refresh the reader's memory, a statement is a complete thought or idea in a sentence. In all, the *Calgary Herald* had the largest number of statements, 318. This was followed by *Le Devoir*, 148; the *Globe and Mail*, 116; *Le Téléjournal*, 50; *The National*, 50; and CTV, 15. This resulted in a total of 697 statements. All subsequent references to percentage in the chapter are of the statement base.

OVERVIEW OF COVERAGE

As Conrad Black complained at the time, there was little media attention devoted to the question of partition during the year we collected our data, even though Black himself made several high-profile speeches arguing in favour of partition of Quebec and a COMPAS poll revealed most Canadians were also in favour of the partition of Quebec, in the event of a "yes" vote in a sovereignty referendum.

Among the news outlets examined, the *Calgary Herald* devoted almost half the coverage of all news outlets combined (46 percent) to the issue of partition. *Le Devoir*, the news outlet with the second-highest volume of coverage, at 21 percent had less than half the coverage of the *Calgary Herald*. The national paper, the *Globe and Mail*, had the third-highest amount of attention, some 17 percent of the total.

Most of the discussion surrounding the question of partition of Quebec was held during the 1997 federal election campaign. Thirty-five percent of the news attention during the year we examined this question focused on the election. However, there were differences between news outlets. While 74 percent of *Le Téléjournal*, 60 percent of all *CTV News*, and 83 percent of *Le Devoir* focused their attention on the question during the election campaign, it was the impetus for coverage in only 48 percent of *The National*, 9 percent of the *Globe and Mail*, and 12 percent of the *Calgary Herald's* coverage on the question of partition.

Almost half of the coverage of the *Globe and Mail* centred on an op-ed piece by Conrad Black. This coverage included a series of letters to the editor penned by Gordon Gibson and replies by Black. The exchange of letters to the editor began after Black addressed an audience of 2,000 at a meeting hosted by the Toronto Board of Trade. In that speech he argued that in the event of a "yes" vote, Canada "would not surrender its legal title to much of Northern Quebec (Abbate 1997, A1). In his column, Gibson responded by raising an obvious concern: the Canadian army, which among

other things, is the organization upon which the enforcing of Canadian law
and Canadian sovereignty ultimately depend, would after separation contain
a large number of foreign, Quebec nationals. Since it would be difficult to
enforce Canadian sovereignty in northern Quebec using the army as a means
to do so, Gibson sided with Tom Kierans who argued that it would be best
not to bother fighting the battle at all. In Gibson's words, it was best to
"minimize the transaction costs" and get down to negotiating a settlement
(Gibson 1997, A15). Black, not satisfied with the "transaction cost minimiza-
tion" argument, describing it as a "good-natured but glib consideration of
Canada's most important problem," fired back with his own pressing questions in the event of a "yes" vote (Black 1997, A19). Gibson responded in
turn and thus ended the most vigorous debate the country had on the question of Quebec partition for the entire year.

Notwithstanding the high-profile Black-Gibson exchange in the *Globe
and Mail,* the *Calgary Herald* had the highest frequency of stories on partition
and the greatest variety of stories related to partition. The *Calgary Herald* did
not limit itself to Conrad Black's comments, but also discussed the issue in
the context of Quebec municipal resolutions on partition, the COMPAS
poll, and the one-year anniversary of the referendum.

Not only was coverage on this issue given little overall attention, but
when it was discussed, it was done in general terms. Researchers identified
the context in which the issue was placed. This variable was called "aspect."
All but *The National* and *Le Téléjournal* discussed the issue in general terms.
For *The National,* the most important consideration of discussion was politics (64 percent). For *Le Téléjournal* it was legal issues, which comprised
40 percent of its overall coverage. This finding clearly illustrates the fact that
the public broadcaster is not a monolith, but that there is diversity in the
Crown corporation between French- and English-language sections, at least
on this issue. The divide is not only ideological, in the sense that anglophone
CBC staff support federalism and francophones support separatism, but the
two language units focus on different issues. Radio-Canada emphasized le-
galities and English-language CBC emphasized political negotiation. That
different foci were presented to their respective audiences indicates how even
when the same topic is discussed, the perspective conveyed may be fundamentally different, depending on the news outlet that examines it and, perhaps, on the individual views of the journalists that constitute the organization.

Reporter statements constituted 39 percent of the total. This ranged from lows of 26 percent for *Le Téléjournal* and 27 percent for *CTV News,* to 58 percent for the *Globe and Mail.* The second most frequent source was the Quebec provincial government, which was the source of 19 percent of all statements. Surprisingly, it was the *Calgary Herald* that provided the most quotes from this source. At the same time, the western daily gave federal government representatives only 7 percent of the coverage – the same as municipal politicians. In contrast, *Le Devoir* gave the federal opposition 24 percent of the attention and the federal government 16 percent. The Quebec government accounted for only 3 percent of sources' statements. This was less than that of interest groups (11 percent). The *Globe and Mail* gave a considerable proportion of its coverage to Conrad Black (15 percent). *The National* and *Le Téléjournal* spread out the comments more evenly between sources, each giving the federal government politicians more coverage than provincial politicians. Part of the reason Quebec provincial politicians were given so little opportunity to discuss the issue was that most of the discussion on these television programs resulted from the federal election campaign. As a consequence, when partition was discussed it was framed more as part of the election event than as a subject worthy of discussion on its own account.

In the 26 May 1997 *Le Devoir,* for example, the movement of the parties and their position was expressed thus: "Jean Chrétien dismissed the debate by saying it was hypothetical. Jean Charest continues to speak about a post-referendum 'Yes' vote as a 'black hole.' Gilles Duceppe, with his allies in Québec, rejects any reference to partition, recognizing all the same that the cases of the natives are disconcerting. In fact, only Preston Manning is presented as sympathetic to the objective of the partitionists, but the latter say they are unable to support him because of the Reform position on official bilingualism and provincial autonomy regarding cultural matters" (Dion 1997).

In the initial content analysis, coders identified in detail the argument that was being presented on the issue of partition. The detailed nature of their coding, however, made it very difficult to capture the general direction of the debate. As a result, many of the substantive arguments for and against partition went uncoded. That is, the initial coding instrument was far too sophisticated or finely calibrated for the level of data that was needed for the study. The four original coding variables of "partition of Canada," for and against, and "partition of Quebec," for and against, yielded 133 statements constituting only 19 percent of the data set. On reading the stories for general trends it was decided that statements should be identified in general terms whether they were arguing in favour of or against Quebec partition, for whatever reason. Recoding the statements into this yes/no category yielded a total of 677 statements reflecting 97 percent of the total. As a result, the original detailed coding of this question was abandoned in favour of a more general set of coding categories

On the question of whether regions in Quebec had the right to separate in the advent of a "yes" vote in a Quebec referendum, the news outlets divided along linguistic lines. English-language CBC provided 58 percent of the arguments on the "yes" side, while the self-described national newspaper, the *Globe and Mail,* provided roughly balanced arguments. For example, in a 29 January 1997 story, Conrad Black's statements on partition were contrasted with comments by Premier Bouchard:

> Mr. Black also said that the rest of Canada should back partitionists in Québec if the sovereigntists were to win a referendum, and argued that successive Quebec governments had unfairly treated Anglophones in the province.
>
> Mr. Bouchard dismissed Mr. Black's comments. "It's a provocation," the Premier said. "It's obviously a desperate attempt to counter Quebec democracy. It is an admission of defeat. It means that Canada will give up trying to convince Quebeckers to stay within the federation by democratic arguments and that the only way to stop democracy in Quebec is to do something like partition," Mr. Bouchard said (Seguin 1997, A5).

Le Téléjournal overwhelmingly provided "no" arguments. In contrast, the *Calgary Herald* and the private national broadcaster, CTV, provided proportionately more "yes" than "no" arguments. *Le Devoir* was also almost balanced in its coverage, with 55 percent of the statements arguing the "no" position.

IDEOLOGICAL CONGRUENCE

Do the opinions held by journalists on the issue of partition predict how the news outlets will report on the issue? To answer this question we return again to the survey results. In the survey, we asked the reporters, "In your view, would regions within Quebec have the right to decide whether they wish to go with Quebec or stay with Canada?" In the survey, 85 percent of English-speaking journalists said "yes," 6 percent said "no," and 8 percent said "don't know." In contrast, 33 percent of French-speaking journalists said "yes," 53 percent said "no," and 15 percent did not know. Statistically, these results were significant at the 0.001 level, which is to say they were highly significant.

The content analysis was remarkably similar. Two-thirds (67 percent) of English-language news outlets presented arguments that favoured the partition of Quebec and 33 percent presented arguments against partition of Quebec. Francophone news outlets presented the "no" opinion view 60 percent of the time and the "yes" opinion 40 percent of the time.

SUMMARY AND DISCUSSION

To summarize the findings of this chapter:

1 There was little coverage paid to the issue of Quebec partition. The *Calgary Herald* provided the most attention, followed by *Le Devoir.*
2 When partition was discussed, it was presented as an election story.
3 English-language CBC, the *Globe and Mail,* and *Le Devoir* were the news organizations most likely to provide both sides of the issue, with CBC and the *Globe and Mail* slightly favouring the "yes" side and *Le Devoir* slightly in favour of the "no" side. The *Calgary Herald* and *Le Téléjournal* were the most unbalanced in their coverage, with the *Calgary Herald* coverage overwhelmingly in support of partition and *Le Téléjournal* arguing the opposite most of the time.
4 Comparing reporter opinions on partition with content analysis revealed that the personal opinion of journalists on partition is reflected in news coverage. Both opinions and aggregate content data were statistically significant with respect to the question of partition when compared with language.

This chapter has identified differences along linguistic lines in the coverage of one national unity issue — that of the partition of Quebec in the event of a "yes" result. These results strongly suggest that to predict how a news outlet will report on national unity issues, one need look no further than the language spoken by the reporter. While in the previous chapter we found the principal cleavages to be between public and private ownership, here we find the principal cleavage to be between language groups. While none of this is surprising, this is the first time we have been able to demonstrate these beliefs in a robust statistical fashion. The data are unequivocal and statistically significant, illustrating once again that journalists matter and that their opinions do influence the news product.

The following chapter examines coverage of Supreme Court decisions on social issues, to see whether journalists' views in this area are also reflected in the news they report.

CHAPTER 8

THE COURTS AND SOCIAL ISSUES

WHY THE COURTS?

The difficulty with trying to analyze media coverage of social issues is deciding which issue to measure. Given the enormous field for action by the embedded Canadian state in the already broad area of social issues, it is necessary to focus attention on a few policies. It is not, however, obvious which social policies are most important, particularly because they all have so many devoted and articulate advocates. In order to find a principle of selection that cannot easily be criticized as being an arbitrary result of the interests of the authors, we decided to proceed inductively. Because of the impact of the Charter of Rights and Freedoms, and because of the political significance of what has been called the "court party" (Knopff and Morton 1992; Morton and Knopff 2000), we decided to examine what the Canadian courts have determined to be important social issues, and to analyze media coverage of these decisions, particularly decisions made by the Supreme Court of Canada. In fact, as we shall see, Supreme Court decisions are important in their own right and have the added advantage of reflecting social policy issues.

It has long been argued that the US Supreme Court has been a catalyst for social change. One has only to look at the landmark decisions such as *Brown* v. *The Board of Education of Topeka* or *Roe* v. *Wade* to see evidence of the impact of court decisions on public policy. For example, the late Thurgood Marshall, the chief litigator for the plaintiff in *Brown* who was subsequently elevated to the US Supreme Court, predicted at the time that desegregation would be complete in five years as a result of the *Brown* decision (Rosenberg 1991). Many others have acknowledged the positive effect of the courts in bringing about social change (Levin 1964). Popular wisdom as represented by the media also appears to be convinced of the power of the courts to effect social change. For example, when Justice Harry Blackmun retired from the US Supreme Court on 6 April 1994, David Halton on *CBC Prime Time News* remembered him as the "man who wrote the court's landmark *Roe* v. *Wade* decision, that women have a fundamental right to abortion." For television viewers that night, the meaning of his long and distinguished career was reduced to a single opinion on a single case.

In addition to litigants and the media, legal scholars contend that not only are the courts powerful agents of change, but that bringing about social change by way of court decisions is both legitimate and important. As Lawrence Tribe states: "In every aspect of our lives ... not even the most passive, restrained, low-profile Supreme Court imaginable can any longer avoid playing a decisive role" (Tribe 1985, 139-40). After the entrenchment of the Canadian Charter of Rights and Freedoms, Alan Gold invoked *Brown* to justify the anticipated role of the Charter. "*Brown*," he writes, "was such a moral supernova in civil liberties adjudication that it almost single-handedly justifies the exercise" (Gold 1982, 108). Similarly, John Whyte declared, "As a matter of principle we have adopted the notion that there are adjudicable public issues" (Whyte 1990, 351).

Interest groups are also convinced that the courts are an effective arena in which they can pursue their agenda. Political scientist Christopher Manfredi (1993, 171) noted that the Women's Legal Education and Action Fund (LEAF), the National Citizens' Coalition (NCC), and the Canadian Civil Liberties Association have been the most active groups launching Charter cases. Organizations are being formed every year in order to raise money and mount Charter challenges. In August 1994, gay and lesbian groups formed a defence fund in preparation for the battle over spousal benefits and adoption rights. In the 1 August 1994 *CBC Prime Time News* report, Brian Stewart noted, "Same-sex couples hope the courts will do what the provincial government would not." A year later, twelve welfare recipients joined to challenge the Ontario government's reduction in welfare funding. They claimed that the reduction violated two sections of the Charter (*Globe and Mail*, 11 November 1995, A1). More recently still, farmers have challenged the monopoly of the Canadian Wheat Board on the grounds (among others) that it violates their Charter-guaranteed freedom of association by compelling them to associate against their will.

One reason groups go to court is to publicize a grievance. Law professor Joel Handler argues that a high-profile case can legitimize a group in the eyes of the media, but also in the eyes of other social and legal élites. A favourable decision repels a political attack because it justifies the group's position: "Law reformers and foundations feel the need for legitimatization for courts ... Cases, particularly when they stop a bulldozer or unmask some outrageous practice, can be dramatic and newsworthy, and provide legitimacy so necessary for support from élites" (1978, 38). When the court option is there, it will be used. Another reason groups go to the courts, as James O'Reilly, the executive legal officer of the Supreme Court, noted, is because "the publicity feeds the perception of a serious, sober look at social process." Court proceedings provide a "calm way for serious treatment of the issues." Therefore, "if a group can get its case into the Court then it is of national importance."[1]

Examining the actual result that a court decision overturning legislation has on the behaviour of an individual is only one way of measuring the impact of the courts on public opinion. There is also the possibility that a court decision upholding legislation may irritate an interest group or public opinion more generally to such an extent that the irritated party brings pressure to bear on the legislature to change a law. Law professor W.A. Bogart, for example, argues against the conventional wisdom that the promotion of women's equality can be attributed to the courts. In fact, the courts initially opposed it. He shows, however, that the publicity of even a failed application to the court might be used to reverse an objectionable policy through legislative action, provided the interested parties are organized and ingenious. For example, in the case of *Murdoch* v. *Murdoch,* the Supreme Court of Canada ruled that, on divorce, the fact that a farm wife worked on the farm did not give her a claim in partnership regarding the value of the farm property. This clearly meant that farm spouses were not equal "before and under the law," to use the language of section 15(1) of the Charter. Bogart contends that the "lobbying and educating led to legislative action that was much broader than a favourable ruling in *Murdoch* would have been, thus demonstrating how a loss in the courts was a catalyst for broader and long-lasting legislative change" (1994, 138). Bogart also cites favourable editorial coverage in major daily newspapers as evidence of this process.

Leslie Pal and F.L. Morton note in their analysis of *Bliss* v. *Attorney General of Canada* (1986) that even though a Supreme Court of Canada decision will necessarily favour one side or the other, the ultimate resolution of the issues also depends on the determination, organization, resources, and wit of the litigants. Though they did not explicitly mention the media, part of the extra-legal strategy of litigants has been to capture media attention favourable to their cause. When Suzanne Thibaudeau, for example, lost on appeal to the Supreme Court of Canada, Justice Minister Allan Rock promised to make changes to the system of child support payments his government had just finished successfully defending. He credited Thibaudeau on the 25 May 1995 *CTV News:* "Because of her tenacity in sticking with it and seeing this case through the issue has been brought very high on the national agenda."

Likewise, in his analysis of the abortion issue, Morton (1992, 229) argues that the media provide a vital role in bridging the interpretative gap between the technical legal language of the courts and the ordinary language of the public. The public cannot understand, much less participate in, the constitutional debate over abortion or any other public policy issue that becomes entangled in the Charter and the courts. Public understanding depends on – and is thus shaped by – "translation" of Supreme Court proceedings and decisions by the national media into common-sense English or French.

Research on the US Supreme Court shows that most ordinary decisions receive little or no media coverage, but media élites do in fact pay close attention to what they perceive as major or landmark decisions (Bohte et al. 1995). Michael Solimine (1980), for example, concluded that magazine reports on court decisions were "high quality but low quantity." In-depth coverage was in fact given to cases that were considered to be of national importance. David Ericson (1977) had similar conclusions in his analysis of newspaper coverage of the US Supreme Court, as did Richard Davis (1994).

In short, the consensus regarding media coverage of the US Supreme Court is that it tends to be sporadic and devoid of detail. When an important decision is handed down, however, the media could, and do, devote substantive attention to it. Important and landmark Supreme Court decisions in both countries fulfill many of these requirements of newsworthiness and therefore are a good fit for media coverage. Routine ones aren't.

To test how the media report social issues, we initially examined Canadian Supreme Court decisions reported in 1996-7. Since social groups often go to court to resolve public policy problems that for one reason or another legislatures have largely ignored, we expected to have a sample of social issues that by their nature would be diverse, complex, and contentious. Deciding on one or two issues to measure media coverage would be too onerous when it came down to examining the large number of news outlets that we included. By allowing the courts to filter the contentious issues, we would obtain a smaller number of stories but perhaps a more diverse sampling than if we examined every story about, for example, abortion, gay rights, or family policy. To test those assumptions, the expectation of this portion of the study was to find social issues reported through court decisions. Of the decisions handed down, we expected more attention to be paid to contentious social issues than commercial or technical legal decisions. Based on the survey results reported above, we expected that journalists would provide favourable coverage to homosexual rights, women's rights, and in general to the liberalization of social institutions.

RESULTS

We conducted a content analysis of 48 *Globe and Mail,* 48 *Calgary Herald,* 44 *Le Devoir,* 6 *CTV News,* 10 CBC *The National,* 1 *The National Magazine,* and 6 *Le Téléjournal* and *Le Point* stories from 1 July 1996 to 30 June 1997, for a total of 163 stories. All stories appearing in each news outlet for the specified period were coded. Again, therefore, the observed sample represents a total population rather than a random or constructed sample. Several tests of intercoder reliability were conducted throughout the procedure and again the results of these tests indicate an acceptable percentage of coder agreement. The intercoder relative score for the Supreme Court study was high, at 84 percent.

PRELIMINARY ANALYSIS

Of the 163 stories on Supreme Court decisions reported in the year we examined, the most coverage came from newspapers. Television gave even less attention to Supreme Court decisions than did newspapers. *The National* provided the most attention, with 290 statements in 10 stories. This distribution between newspapers and television is consistent with American media coverage of the US Supreme Court.

The assumption of this study is that media coverage of Supreme Court decisions will reflect media attention to social issues. The problem with this assumption is that in the 1996-7 time frame, the Supreme Court did not rule on any major social issue. We discuss this problem under "Secondary Analysis," below. The first thing to note, however, is that, as a result of relatively few decisions on contentious social issues, some observers concluded – as it happened, prematurely – that courts were growing more deferential to legislatures. Commenting on the quantity of Supreme Court decisions in 1996, Patrick Monahan and Michael Bryant (1997), for example, titled their *Canada Watch* article, "The Supreme Court of Canada's 1996 Constitutional Cases: The End of Charter Activism?" Considering the dearth of contentious social issues, a more appropriate question might be why the Supreme Court received any coverage at all in our time frame. To find out which cases were covered and why, we conducted a regression analysis of the 134 decisions that were handed down by the Supreme Court in 1996-7. In addition, we looked at 5 socially controversial cases on the go that year and included them in the regression model (several of these cases are discussed under "Secondary Analysis," below).

The regression analysis follows a similar model developed by Elliot Slotnick and Jennifer Segal, who examined the same relationship for the American Supreme Court's 1989 term (1998). Media attention to decisions reported during the 1996-7 term (plus the five controversial cases) were the source of the dependent variable. The independent variables were measured from analysis of the cases described in the Supreme Court.

Dependent Variable
The purpose of this analysis is to understand why some rulings are reported and others are not. This will help explain, in part, why media attention to the

Supreme Court was minimal in 1996-7. To that end, the dependent variable is the amount of attention to the case decision. The variables ranged from no coverage (coded zero) to significant attention having more than 100 statements (coded three). The fundamental question here is whether the case was reported at all.

Independent Variables

The independent variables in the model include measures that are case specific and/or institutionally determined (such as number of intervenors, government involvement, and case vote), as well as those that tap media constraints and notions of newsworthiness (such as the issue of the case). Some of the variables examined by Slotnick and Segal cannot be applied to the Canadian context, and were excluded. For example, they identified the decision date as an important variable. They note that the American Supreme Court provides a disproportional number of decisions at the end of the court's term. The remaining cases are announced more sporadically and unpredictably throughout the remainder of the court's session. While it may be true that this signals American journalists that cases delivered at the end of the term are more important, the Canadian Supreme Court does not deliver cases in the same way so we did not include this variable.

In addition, the number of cases announced on the same decision day seemed counter-intuitive. Slotnick and Segal argued that if many decisions were delivered on the same day, there would be less time to cover those cases, which seems to contradict their previous argument that decisions should be seen as more important if they are delivered at the end of term. In any event, this variable was also irrelevant to Canadian court procedures, as was the issue of lower courts. According to Slotnick and Segal, journalists felt that some lower courts were more important than others. This variable did not apply to our sample because most cases come to the Supreme Court by way of provincial appellate courts and no lower court is able to direct a case to the Supreme Court.

The full model for this study includes the following variables:

1 *Cohesion of judges:* An obvious indicator of conflict in Supreme Court decisions is the final vote. This reflects the degree to which there is disagreement among the justices. As did Slotnick and Segal, we assume that

the greater division, the more likely the media would pay attention to the case. Conflict was measured with a five-point scale, ranging from unanimous vote (coded zero) to a highly divided vote (5-4, 4-3, coded four). In between these extremes are the possibility of a highly cohesive (8-1, 7-1, 6-1, or 5-1, coded one), a moderately cohesive (7-2, 6-2, or 5-2, coded two), and a moderately divided (6-3, 5-3, or 4-2, coded as three) vote.

2 *Federal government involvement in a case:* While there are no beat reporters for the Supreme Court, most media outlets employ journalists to cover Parliament. The emphasis on federal politics and the federal government is evident with the large proportion of the news hole that they fill. We expect that the involvement of the federal government in a case signals to reporters covering the court and politics that the case represents a potentially important instance of litigation, with a greater level of government involvement increasing the likelihood of coverage. The measure of government involvement ranges from no involvement (coded as zero) to being a direct party in the litigation (coded as two). In between these two possibilities the federal government may have acted as an intervenor (coded as one).

3 *Total number of intervenors:* As noted above, interest group participation in the judicial process has been a way for groups to place their claims high on the national agenda. The most common form of interest group activity in the courts has been to obtain intervenor status. The number of such intervenors should signal to journalists that a court case is contentious or deals with significant matters. The expectation is that the higher the number of intervenors, the more media attention a case receives. We measured the number of intervenors by intervals of five, with zero indicating no intervenors, one indicating up to five intervenors, two indicating up to ten, and so on. If there were more than twenty-five intervenors in a case, it was coded as six.

4 *Issue area of case:* Certain news stories attract greater media attention than others. The more the story fulfills journalistic needs for conflict, drama, and interesting visuals, the more likely a story will appear in the news. So too do court cases have varying degrees of conflict, drama, and interest. The Supreme Court of Canada provides the issue area of the case in its reasons for judgment. We categorized issues according to economic (including taxation, commerce), criminal, constitutional, and Aboriginal. All

these issue areas were included as dummy variables in the model, with each case coded as one if it involved the issue and zero if it did not. These variables were similar to those of Slotnick and Segal. However, we believe that Slotnick and Segal failed to acknowledge that controversial social issues might warrant attention on their own merits. We note that the Slotnick–Segal regression analysis yielded an adjusted R^2 of .297, indicating that only about 30 percent of the variance in the dependent variable could be explained by the independent variables. We added a variable that reflects the degree of controversy surrounding an issue to show cases that had received significant media attention in the past might boost the coverage of the case. These cases were coded in the same way as the ones delivered in the 1996-7 court year. The added controversial cases were those cases that received significant media attention the year before our analysis and the year after. They were *Vriend* v. *Alberta, Thibaudeau* v. *Canada, Egan* v. *Canada, M.* v. *H.,* and *RJR-MacDonald Inc.* v. *Canada (Attorney General).*

5 *Upheld or dismissed:* Another source of drama for deciding whether or not to report a Supreme Court story is whether the judgment of a lower court was upheld or dismissed. Cases that were upheld hold less drama and excitement than those that are dismissed. Court rulings that resulted in upholding the lower court decision were coded as zero, while those dismissing or quashing the decision were coded as one.

The regression analysis yielded an adjusted R^2 value of 0.355 indicating that 36 percent of the variance in coverage can be explained by the independent variables. The three variables that statistically were highly significant were the involvement of intervenors, controversy, and whether it was upheld or dismissed. The involvement of intervenors provided the greatest predictor for media coverage. The more intervenors a case attracted, the more likely the case would be covered by the media. As expected, our controversy variable provides more explanation of the coverage of the case holding all other variables constant. We found a negative correlation between the decision of the case and its media attention.

The cohesion of the judges provides little explanation for variance in media coverage. Similarly, the amount of federal government involvement seemed to provide little explanation for coverage either. This analysis thus supports our initial suspicion that the media will report on Supreme Court decisions if there is a controversial social issue, but it does not provide us with any assessment of how the media covered social issues.

The only series of cases that can give us an approximate indication of media attention to social issues concerns the Aboriginal cases heard during the court year. In our survey of journalists, we canvassed their views on a variety of groups and their opinion of the respect those groups received. One group of particular importance was Aboriginal leaders.

The mode for Aboriginal leaders was 5, with 31 percent of journalists placing the respect they received as being just slightly above the middle value. Fifty percent of the journalists placed their opinions of Aboriginal leaders above the middle value of 4, with 30 percent placing it below the middle mark. The mean for journalists on the question was 4.4, indicating a moderate view of the respect owed Aboriginal leaders. The mean for the public was the same. There were no differences between French- and English-speaking journalists, nor were there any differences between private- and public-sector journalists. The one-sample t-test yielded a value of 68.930. In the independent t-tests there were no statistical differences between French- and English-speaking journalists or between public- and private-sector journalists. This finding leads us to the expectation that coverage of Aboriginal cases in all news outlets would be balanced, but slightly more supportive of Aboriginal peoples because of the support for Aboriginal leaders expressed in the opinion poll.

Coverage of Aboriginal cases confirms this expectation. Detailed statements on Aboriginal court cases were recoded into a three-value variable, with one indicating positive attention to the Aboriginal case, two indicating information, and three indicating negative attention to the case. The bulk (80 percent) of the attention was neutral and factual descriptions of the case. Of the remainder, twice as many statements were pro-Aboriginal as opposed to reporting statements that were critical of the Aboriginal parties.

This is somewhat surprising since three of the five cases ended in the appeal being dismissed. What is more surprising is that only two of the five cases resulted in the negative comments: *R. v. Gladstone* and *R. v. Van der Peet*. The first, *Gladstone,* resulted in the appeal being allowed. Only five statements provided assessments critical of the Aboriginal position. In *Van der*

Peet, the appeal was dismissed. Nine percent of the coverage was critical of the Aboriginal position. Neither of the other two cases that resulted in dismissal provided negative assessments of the Aboriginal position. Therefore, as expected, coverage of the Aboriginal position was presented in a slightly supportive manner by Canadian journalists.

SECONDARY ANALYSIS

As we indicated above, 1996 was not a year during which a large number of significant Supreme Court of Canada decisions on social issues were made. Some of the most significant rulings from the Supreme Court on social issues, however, and ones that were covered in great detail by the news media, occurred a year before and a year after the time during which this study was conducted. Accordingly, in order to examine news coverage of the court's decisions in this important area of social policy, we expanded our time horizons. In a preliminary study of television coverage of the Supreme Court of Canada we found that the cases CBC and CTV focused on in 1995 were *Thibaudeau, Egan,* and *RJR MacDonald.* The major case dealing with a significant social issue after 1996 was *Vriend.* Here we describe how television news covered the 1995 cases and how the *Globe and Mail* and *Calgary Herald* covered *Vriend* in 1997. This selection does not capture the francophone media; it provides a more limited analysis of how journalists' views on social issues are reflected in the news covered.

The issue in *Thibaudeau* was whether a provision of the Income Tax Act, that custodial parents include child support payments in their taxable incomes while non-custodial parents claim the payments as a deduction, violated section 15 equality guarantees in the Canadian Charter of Rights and Freedoms. Suzanne Thibaudeau argued that the provisions discriminated against her as a single custodial parent and contributed to the high poverty rates among female-headed, single-parent families in Canada. The government countered that the policy helped single-parent families because usually it allowed the parent in the lower tax bracket to pay tax on income earned by the parent in the higher tax bracket, which constituted a tax saving to the post-divorce unit as a whole. When the ruling came down on 25 May 1995, both CBC and CTV noted that the Supreme Court "split right along gender lines" in reaching its decision. The five male justices who heard the case disagreed with Thibaudeau, while Justices Beverley McLachlin and Claire L'Heureux-Dubé agreed with Thibaudeau.

CBC paid an overwhelming amount of attention to the arguments put forward by Thibaudeau and her supporters. The predictable result was a very one-sided portrayal of the case. Statements aired on CBC were three times as likely to support Thibaudeau's arguments as criticize them. Thirty percent of CBC's overall coverage of *Thibaudeau* was neutral. Of the remaining statements, 53 percent were supportive of Thibaudeau, but only 18 percent sided with the government.

CTV's coverage of *Thibaudeau* was a great contrast to that of CBC. CTV aired the same proportion of neutral statements as CBC, but it provided nearly twice as many statements supporting the government's position as it did in support of Thibaudeau. It has become something of a journalistic convention for reporters to avoid making direct evaluative statements or clear indications of their own opinions and preferences on a particular issue. Instead, they usually select sources with strong views supporting or opposing an issue, person, or the significance of an event or action. This makes for dramatic reporting, and selection of sources with strong but contrasting views maintains the appearance of neutrality – though, of course, the actual selection can also influence the spin given to a story. What is remarkable in media coverage of *Thibaudeau,* however, is that anchors and reporters strayed from this convention and offered their own assessments of the case. Although the majority of both CBC and CTV statements by reporters were neutral (59 percent on CBC and 60 percent on CTV), the balance of their assessments clearly supported the position of Thibaudeau. Anchors and reporters were nine times more likely on CBC and twice as likely on CTV to be complimentary than critical of Suzanne Thibaudeau's arguments. For example, CBC's Tom Kennedy gloomily reported on 25 May 1995, "For Canadians who object to the court's decision, there is no more legal recourse. As for Thibaudeau, she now says unless the tax laws are changed, thousands of single parents in this country will be stuck in a state of poverty."

And perhaps CTV's Paula Newton already had a compromise solution in mind when she asserted on *CTV News* for 25 May 1995: "Canadian families will be looking for a little balance between those who say the system works and those like Suzanne Thibaudeau who say the system takes much needed money away from their kids." There was, of course, balanced coverage in many of the reports, but it is worth noting that the source of balance was found less in journalists' assessments than in those from the sources themselves. On CTV, the balanced sources were legal experts. On CBC, however, those from interest groups outnumbered statements from the legal experts. Even the criticisms of Thibaudeau's position were contrasted with the views of a large contingent of interest groups, the arguments of whom favoured her case nine times out of ten. The law professors and lawyers featured on the networks provided some critical balance (18 percent of CBC and 42 percent of CTV statements were critical of Thibaudeau's legal arguments). Legal experts made 65 percent of the negative comments on CBC, and 60 percent of the negative comments on CTV. Even then, Patrick Monahan of Osgoode Hall and Jack London of the University of Manitoba, who provided the majority of these statements, were noticeably half-hearted in their criticisms. London simply remarked on *CTV News* for 25 May 1995, "Men obviously have more power than women do in our society, Lloyd [Robertson], and in these cases, the women judges have shown themselves to be the more liberal than the men, but that's a bad rap in this case. This case wasn't about that; this case was about the fairness in the tax system, and the Court probably came to the right conclusion. This wasn't about men against women. The Court probably arrived at the right decision."

The second 1995 case that received considerable television attention was *Egan,* which involved a challenge by a homosexual couple on the definition of "spouse" in Old Age Security legislation. This legislation prevents same-sex couples from qualifying for spousal benefits. In *Egan,* the claimant argued that his exclusion from the benefit scheme constituted discrimination on the basis of sexual orientation.

Although television news provided substantially favourable attention to the position of Thibaudeau, they were even more supportive of Egan's position. On both networks, negative commentary was negligible. Half of CBC and 40 percent of CTV coverage of the *Egan* case was neutral. Of the remainder, almost all the statements on both networks were supportive of Egan. The most negative analysis of the *Egan* case came from law professor Jack London, who was not critical of Egan himself, but rather of the Court.

On the 25 May 1995 *CTV News,* Professor London said, "Essentially, what they're saying is, it's the old saw, political saw, Lloyd, about being a fiscal conservative and a social liberal. The Court's saying yes to liberalism for homosexuality, they are entitled to protection, but not when it costs money. That's the bottom line."

Unlike the coverage of Suzanne Thibaudeau's case, reporters and anchors offered very little assessment of *Egan.* Most of their comments were factual. The bulk of the positive commentary about *Egan* came from interest groups and legal experts. In fact, only on CTV did any source dissent from the dominant opinion. The only negative evaluation of Egan's argument, provided by Jim Weisgerber of the Catholic Bishops Conference, was quoted briefly on the 25 May 1995 *CTV News.* Weisgerber stated that spouses are married people and "marriage is between a man and a woman."

Despite their factual presentation of the case, television journalists were quick to point out that Egan won more for gay rights than he lost. Peter Mansbridge, in introducing a story on the 25 May 1995 CBC *Prime Time News,* said, "Egan has lost his own case, but won a victory for all homosexuals." Ian Hanomansing added in the story immediately following, "At least one legal analyst who has studied the decision says too much is being made of what Egan and Nesbitt lost – the specific benefit – [and] not enough of what they won." Thus Egan was said to have won a moral victory because the courts decided that homosexuality could be the basis for sexual discrimination. The story was then refocused on the likely consequences of the decision, that it established a precedent that would open the doors for later cases involving equality rights for gay men and lesbians. Lloyd Robertson in his 25 May 1995 newscast said, "The high court said, 'no, homosexual couples cannot collect the same pension benefits that other couples receive.' But in making that ruling, it said 'discrimination against homosexuals is against the law.' So, as Roger Smith reports, gays and lesbians are left with something to cheer about, and reason to be unhappy." CTV then showed a clip of John Fraser, a "gay rights activist," saying, "We know that we are equal. Nothing can change that. The Supreme Court has opened the doors to future legal challenges."

In the CBC panel discussion presented on 25 May 1995 on the *Prime Time Magazine,* the two commentators, Patrick Monahan from Osgoode Hall Law School and Shelagh Day from the National Action Committee on the Status of Women, were very critical of the majority ruling in *Egan.*

Indeed, the opinions of these two panellists formed a united front. This lineup of opinion also goes somewhat against the usual practices, at least as they are outlined on paper, at the CBC. In theory, CBC panels provide contrasting or opposed opinions so as to indicate they are living up to the ever-elusive norm of "balance." It seems obvious to common sense that, if two people with contrasting opinions cannot be found for the same program, then it is redundant to interview two individuals with the same opinion. In this case, however, the commentators merely echoed each other. For example, Monahan remarked,

> When you read the judgement as a whole, I think the sense you get is that the court is taking a very narrow approach to the overall burden of justification, if you will, that's on government in order to justify laws that might discriminate against gays and lesbians. I mean, essentially, I think the court is saying that it's open to Parliament and to the legislatures to prefer heterosexual couples because of the ability of heterosexual couples to procreate and have children. And I must say, for my money, on this one, I think the court got it wrong. I must say I found the dissenting judgement, judgements, in fact, much more persuasive here.

To which Day responded, "And I agree again. It seems to me we've got a real question here that the court, the majority, is just not dealing with properly – what is the basis for social benefits in our society?"

By providing two commentators with essentially the same position, CBC obviously failed to provide an alternative perspective. In *Thibaudeau*, the commentators acknowledged that another side of the argument did exist, namely, that Thibaudeau could have had her child support reduced if her husband could not make the deduction from his support payment. However, with *Egan*, commentators did not acknowledge that there was another side to the case. In fact, there was: because Egan and his partner had been paying taxes as individuals rather than as a couple, because they were, therefore, not considered a couple for tax purposes, they could each qualify for tax benefits such as GST credits, something that a combined income might preclude them from doing. In examining only the benefits to heterosexuals, television painted an overly rosy picture of how the tax system benefits opposite-sex couples.

RJR MacDonald Inc. v. *Canada* was a challenge by a tobacco manufacturer to Canada's ban on tobacco advertising. In *RJR,* the claimant tobacco company argued that the tobacco advertising ban violated its freedom of expression under the Charter. The appeal was successful, and the Supreme Court struck down the ban against tobacco advertising on 21 September 1995.

Television provided more neutral descriptions of the *RJR* case than they did of *Egan* or of *Thibaudeau.* Almost one-fifth of CBC and one-quarter of CTV statements about the tobacco ban case were neutral. However, while television's attention to Thibaudeau's argument was twenty-five times more likely to be positive than negative, and while attention to Egan's argument was entirely positive, attention to RJR's arguments was favourable in only 19 percent of CBC's and 21 percent of CTV's overall attention to this case. Examining the balance of opinion, CBC was twice as likely and CTV almost twice as likely to criticize as to support the Supreme Court's decision.

The trend favouring Thibaudeau and Egan and criticizing RJR was evident even when one examines journalists' statements in isolation. CBC journalists were eight times more likely to be critical of RJR's arguments than to support them. In contrast, journalists on CTV were only slightly more negative than positive toward the ruling. CTV reporters focused on the fact that the tobacco industry was going to be self-regulating. For example, on 21 September 1995, Roger Smith of CTV emphasized, "Despite its victory, the tobacco industry promised to live by the old rules while it talks to the government about new, less restrictive ones."

CBC coverage focused more on the moral issue of smoking. For example, Dan Bjarnason on the CBC *Magazine* on 21 September 1995 had this to say about tobacco advertising: "What now seems so wrong with this picture is that there was a time when nothing was wrong with this picture. The ordinariness of smoking was the problem. Cigarette advertising was so pervasive and so overwhelming; it convinced many of us into believing smoking was so very normal. Why did those people blitz us like that? University of Toronto historian and author Paul Rutherford cautions us, don't believe the tobacco propaganda." The subsequent discussion on the *Magazine* was often acrimonious and heated when tobacco lobbyist Rob Parker of the Canadian Tobacco Manufacturers Association was pitted against Michael Dector, who was labelled a health care policy analyst. It was obvious whose interests Parker represented, but what of Dector? Parker argued his case on legal grounds, but the debate often moved away from the law to the issue of health risks. Thus Parker argued, "The industry's pleased about the result. I think it's not only a victory for freedom of expression. It's a victory for common sense ... It's a coup in – a victory – they believe they have a fundamental right to communicate with their customers, they make and sell a legal product." Dector's arguments emphasized the need for bans and increased taxation on tobacco products. He also argued that the industry is very powerful. He said, for example,

> It's very hard to pull it down. It's very hard to pull down smoking. The industry is very successful in finding ways to identify with worthwhile causes, to identify with sports events, to identify with worthwhile causes, to identify in its naming of products with the problems young women have with self-esteem. It's a very tough issue to change your behaviour of people with an addictive substance. This isn't freedom of choice. This isn't some substance people get up in the morning to say, "Well I'll think I'll make a decision." This is a highly addictive substance that an industry makes a lot of money from. And that makes it unique and it's why the entire health community in this country stand against your industry and stand against anything that gets in the way of trying to reduce the consumption of tobacco.

It is clear enough that a debate between spokespeople for the smoking lobby and the health lobby provides for good television entertainment, but *RJR* was chiefly about freedom of speech, and television coverage did not examine the Court's decision with respect to this issue. What distinguished the coverage of *RJR* from *Thibaudeau* or *Egan* was that, with respect to *RJR*, legal analysts were conspicuously absent. There was little discussion about the majority and dissenting opinions. No analysis was offered of the arguments presented by the justices, and no assessments were made about the composition and biases of those sitting on the Supreme Court. Further, unlike *Thibaudeau* and *Egan,* audiences were not told what precedent *RJR* might set, nor told whether the court was justified in its denial of government activity. Television coverage focused on the narrow health and moral issues surrounding the sale and use of tobacco products.

The public policy implications of *Thibaudeau, Egan,* and *RJR* were profound. In all three cases the courts ruled against social change. In all three

cases television news argued for social change. In all three cases, the legislative consequences were closer to the position taken by the media than by
the courts. As a result of these cases, and, we would argue, media coverage of
them, the government has became more active in regulating the relevant
policy areas than they were before the decisions.

In the federal budget handed down in March 1996, for example, the government announced that it would no longer require divorced parents with
custody of their children to pay tax on child support payments from their
ex-spouses. The old rules were said to perpetuate poverty among single
parents, of whom the vast majority are women. The non-custodial parents
would pay the tax instead. According to the *Globe and Mail,* this legislative
change was a direct result of *Thibaudeau:* "The overhaul arises from the long
court battle waged by Susan [sic] Thibaudeau, who went to the Supreme
Court of Canada to argue, unsuccessfully, that having to pay taxes on child-
support payments unfairly penalizes custodial parents" (Ha and McIlroy
1996, A1).

A similar significance attaches to the final case we examined, *Vriend.* On 2
April 1998, the Supreme Court of Canada ruled that Alberta human rights
legislation did not protect homosexuals from discrimination and was thus in
violation of section 15 of the Charter. The decision resulted from Delwin
Vriend's seven-year battle with the Alberta government to have his dismissal
from a private Christian school adjudicated by the Alberta Human Rights
Commission. In the decision, Supreme Court Justices Frank Iacobucci and
Peter Corry argued that the ruling that requires homosexual rights to be
"read in" to Alberta's human rights legislation was not the final stage of the
process. They pointed to section 33 of the Charter, which allowed the Alberta
Legislature to use the so-called notwithstanding clause to override the Supreme Court decision. By implication at least, the court was initiating what
has since become known as a "dialogue theory" of the relationship between
courts and legislatures wherein the use of section 33 would be pivotal.

Premier Ralph Klein's initial reaction was, "It's pretty hard to go against
that kind of judgment and the kind of consideration which was given ... by
the Supreme Court of Canada." What Mr. Klein did not acknowledge was
that it would be equally difficult to go against the perception of Alberta as a
human rights backwater. In the week following the decision, the premier's

office was deluged with 1,000 phone calls and faxes a day calling for the notwithstanding clause to be used, and for the "dialogue" to commence.

CBC and CTV gave the *Vriend* decision very little coverage. Although it was the lead item on *The National,* their coverage consisted of only one story. No in-depth coverage or discussion of the decision was provided on *The National* or *The National Magazine,* no in-depth interview with the plaintiff, Delwin Vriend, no sharp insights from celebrated legal minds. In short, the coverage was nothing like that given to *Egan* or *Thibaudeau.*

On CBC, the only commentary was in Alison Smith's introductory remarks that the "ruling amounts to rewriting Alberta law to bring it into line with the federal Charter of Rights." This statement carried the implication that the Charter contains a specific clause that identifies and protects gay rights, and so ignores the arguably more significant judicial procedure of "reading in" rights, whereby judges find by implication provision of rights that legislatures either inadvertently or deliberately did not include in the law. In the Alberta human rights legislation, there was no question that the exclusion of gay rights from legal protection had been considered and debated in the legislature and that, as a result of those considerations and debates, gay rights had been deliberately excluded. The lack of discussion on the controversial practice of reading in rights, including gay rights, gives credibility to the perception that Alberta was simply wrong, and that the Alberta human rights laws were simply violations of the Charter. The *Magazine* portion of *The National* on CBC was also silent on the entire procedural issue. The two stories that night were on hepatitis C and a report on a cancer doctor. The next night CBC chose to present its game show *The National Quiz* rather than discuss what has become known as "judicial activism."

CTV News also omitted any discussion of the *Vriend* decision. There was only one story about it the day the decision was brought down, and it was placed second in the news lineup. Again, this is in contrast to *CTV News'* treatment of *Egan,* where it was the lead item and followed up by an interview between Lloyd Robertson and Jack London, the University of Manitoba law professor.

In total, CBC provided only three stories and CTV only two on the *Vriend* decision. The lack of attention by the national television news media implies tacit approval of the Supreme Court's activism. Much of the media's power lies in what they choose to discuss and what to omit. When issues are not debated, the media signal is that there is no controversy, no opposing viewpoints that have merit, and, in this case, certainly no controversial procedural issues. By giving the decision as little attention as they did, and providing practically no debate on judicial activism, which is the pre-eminent procedural issue in the Canadian justice system, these news outlets all signalled their tacit approval of the decision and of judicial activism. In contrast to *Egan* and *Thibaudeau,* where judicial decisions did not accord with the postmaterialist media agenda and so led to intensive scrutiny and analysis, *Vriend* was so clearly in accord with what might be called the media view of the world that any critical appraisal or even a balanced discussion would have been superfluous.

In contrast to television coverage of the *Vriend* decision, the *Calgary Herald* and the *Globe and Mail* gave extensive attention to the decision. Since there was a mixture of news, analysis, and opinion stories on the decision, the remainder of the discussion will contrast the *Herald* with the *Globe* coverage.

Overall, the *Globe and Mail* provided more attention in favour of the decision than against it. While one-quarter of the coverage indicated the facts of the case, 42 percent of the statements argued in favour of the decision and 33 percent were against it. For the *Calgary Herald,* an opposite trend emerged: 18 percent of the overall attention was neutral, while 40 percent was in favour of the decision and slightly more arguments (42 percent) were made against the decision. Part of the difference can be accounted for by the fact that the *Herald* ran more commentary pieces than did the *Globe* and that those commentary stories by such critics of the Supreme Court as F. L. Morton shifted the tone of the overall coverage. Indeed, when we examine statements made by journalists rather than sources or guest opinion pieces, we find that for the *Globe and Mail* 41 percent of the statements are neutral with only 27 percent of the statements in support of the decision and 33 percent against it. Similarly, in the *Herald* 25 percent of the statements were neutral while 36 percent were in favour and 39 percent against the decision.

The reason primarily given in support of the decision was the need for protection of minority groups. A full 27 percent of the reasons stated in the *Globe and Mail* and 33 percent of the reasons in the *Herald* for arguing in favour of the decision came down to the idea that gays needed protection by the law. Another 14 percent of the journalists in the *Globe* and 8 percent in the *Herald* argued that the courts needed to be active in such situations because politicians were afraid to do anything for gays and lesbians.

Arguments against the Court's decision in *Vriend* were not directed against the substance of legal protection of minorities and even less were they in any sense "anti-gay." Rather, the bulk of the criticism was directed against judicial activism. We would interpret this configuration of opinion in terms of the ambivalence or sensitivity to the issue of gay rights in general, which reflects the unease that journalists have in dealing with the issue. It will be recalled from the survey results reported above that, when asked about the amount of attention that gays and lesbians received, journalists were more likely than the general public to say that gays and lesbians did not receive as much attention as they warranted. Very few journalists indicated that gays and lesbians received too much attention. In reporting the *Vriend* decision, journalists balanced their own relatively supportive feelings toward gays and lesbians with reports on advocating the use of the notwithstanding clause, section 33. Very few statements objected to the rights of gays and lesbians, but instead focused on the courts and their role in propelling social change. At the same time there was support of this role of the courts.

SUMMARY AND DISCUSSION

The analysis of media coverage of the Supreme Court decisions may be summarized as follows:

1 Supreme Court decisions were given very little attention in the news media analyzed for the 1996-7 court term.
2 The greatest amount of attention came from the *Globe and Mail* and the *Calgary Herald*.
3 The limited coverage of Supreme Court decisions was a direct result of the court docket for the year analyzed. No decisions in controversial cases were delivered by the court during the time frame analyzed. When, however, the period was expanded to include controversial cases, we found the media tended to advocate or to emphasize postmaterialist perceptions and the desirability of postmaterialist outcomes. Sometimes this took the form of criticizing the court for having reached a "wrong" (i.e., non-postmaterialist) decision and on other occasions the reporting without

commentary indicated that there was not much worthy of criticism, even when other sources indicated a quite different appraisal.

4 A regression analysis of the court cases and various elements of the coverage was conducted and confirmed that, in order for a court case to receive significant media attention, it needs to be considered controversial, to be accompanied by intervenors, and be a split decision.

5 Isolating Aboriginal issues showed that journalist opinion should provide a moderate position on the issues, but at the same time slightly favour the Aboriginal position. Coverage of Aboriginal cases tended to reflect these personal views.

We have thus clearly demonstrated the strong correlation between journalists as opinion leaders and news coverage of social issues. There should be little doubt that journalism is a human endeavour and decisions on what goes in a newspaper or television news program has more to do with the journalists than the owners. Of course, there are all sorts of extraneous reasons why some stories make the news rather than others. Availability of pictures, other events occurring in the day, et cetera, may impact what stories are presented and what are omitted. What this chapter has shown is that, despite the constraints on news personnel, they do have enormous power in what stories to emphasize and what stories to highlight. For television news to give so little attention to the *Vriend* decision, in light of the attention the *Globe and Mail* and *Calgary Herald* provided, is testimony to this point.

Apart from whether or not to run a story, the slant or direction of the coverage is even more at the hands of journalists. While it may be that journalists have limited control on the news lineup for the day, they do have enormous control over the sources that are presented to explain, denounce, or applaud court decisions. In the coverage of the Supreme Court, we find that the pattern of coverage is not − as one would intuitively expect − to provide more attention to the winners over the losers, but to provide more supportive coverage of whomever the media themselves back. This was clear in the coverage of court decisions involving Aboriginal issues, where, despite the losses in the courts, the media presented the arguments in favour of the Aboriginal position. The same held for homosexual issues as in *Egan,* or in family issues such as *Thibaudeau*. The next and final chapter provides some closing thoughts and avenues for further research.

CHAPTER 9

FINDINGS IN A SHIFTING MEDIASCAPE

The results of this study have provided considerable information on how the values of journalists are reflected in the news they report. A significant feature of these data is that coverage of public policy issues in the Canadian media reflects journalists' opinions to a far greater extent than the views that cultural critics presume to be held by managers or owners. Even those views must remain in the netherworld of assumption because, apart from a few conspicuous exceptions (such as Conrad Black, who has treated us to editorials in newspapers he has owned), no one has ever asked publishers and other media moguls what, in fact, they thought about various materialist, let alone postmaterialist, questions. Nor, again with a few conspicuous exceptions, do media owners typically use their access to the newspapers or even to television networks, to inform their readers or their audience of their own opinions.[1]

In this final chapter we wish to do two things: first, to sketch a few conclusions about what we have found, and second, to make explicit the limitations of this study and thereby to indicate questions to be explored in subsequent research.

JOURNALISTS' ROLE IN NEWS COVERAGE

This study began with the observation that journalists are important to study because they are the actual mediators of the media: they play an important as well as an essential role in determining what goes to air or sees print as well as the shape it takes. We examined the research literature to see whether journalists were considered to be active promoters of change or whether they supported the status quo, and although the cultural critics assumed that journalists' beliefs were secondary to the putative wishes and demands of owners, the literature review indicated that journalists themselves ultimately researched, obtained sources for, and wrote their own news stories. Previous surveys of Canadian journalists indicated that they felt autonomous and did not write the news to please their bosses, but to provide a fair and balanced story. But even the most open-minded journalist must make assumptions as to what counts as being worthy of inclusion on the scale that measures balance, to say nothing about when, in fact, a balance point is reached. Our first task, therefore, was to uncover what journalists' political views were. Thus we conducted a survey of journalists and of the public to measure what journalists' political views were and how they felt the owners affected their day-to-day jobs. In addition, we compared journalists' opinions with those of the public. Both French- and English-speaking journalists were surveyed.

Journalists displayed the demographic characteristics expected on the basis of postmaterialist theory. Taken as a group, English-speaking journalists were highly educated, non-religious males, married or living common law, and in their forties. Francophone journalists were married, university educated, had at least one child living at home, and did not identify themselves with any religious denomination. While English-speaking journalists exhibited these characteristics more so than their audience, French-speaking journalists were quite similar to their audience.

On the question of belief in God, both journalist populations were significantly less likely to espouse a strong belief compared with their audiences. These demographic and religious factors lead us to conclude that journalists – especially anglophones – would, following postmaterialist theory, be more interested in "higher-level" problems such as rights-based claims or environmentalism compared with the general population.

On social issues, anglophone journalists provided stronger trends on factor analysis when describing eight groups in society than did the public. In the first component, which we called progressive, English-speaking journalists strongly placed Aboriginal leaders, feminists, environmentalists, and anti-American academics on this dimension. They did so more than the public. For francophone journalists, there was little consistency in the placement of different social groups. However, journalists' opinions were still different from their public. This supported the findings in the analysis of demographics that anglophone journalists would be likely to express postmaterialist values on social issues to a greater extent than the general public and more so than the francophone journalist population.

However, on the abortion question, English- and French-speaking journalists both manifest postmaterialist tendencies stronger than their respective audiences. Journalists were more likely than the population as a whole to express strong support for the moral and legal right to abortion. While anglophones also had stronger support for gays and lesbians than their audiences, French-speaking journalists were less likely to be supportive of these groups.

This leads us to conclude that anglophone journalists hold relatively strong postmaterialist values on social issues. However, francophone journalists cannot be labelled in any consistent manner. One reason for the inability to pigeonhole French-speaking journalists could be the relatively small sample size of this population. In many cases, a sample of fifty-five could not eliminate chance variation for the distribution of cases within the variables. The findings with respect to francophone journalists are evocative and indicate that additional, larger surveys are needed to understand fully the dynamics of this population.

To test whether the value orientations of journalists could be present in the tenor of stories they wrote, we examined media coverage of Supreme Court decisions. Supreme Court decisions were chosen because of the well-documented tendency for interest groups to gain credibility through publicity associated with an important court case. The Supreme Court, it was theorized, would act as our filter for social issues because at the same time it would deal with politically contentious issues, and thus issues important to the media. In this way we would limit the volume of overall social issue coverage in a non-arbitrary way. Unfortunately, the year in which we conducted the larger study was a year when the Supreme Court did not rule on any major social issue. The year before, the Court had ruled on single-parent taxation (*Thibaudeau* v. *Canada*), free speech (*RJR-MacDonald* v. *Canada*), and gay rights (*Egan* v. *Canada*). In the year after our study, the court ruled on gay rights (*Vriend* v. *Alberta*) and gay adoption (*M.* v. *H.*), which suggests that the courts do provide a filter for how the media cover contentious social issues.

When we examined *Thibaudeau, RJR, Egan,* and *Vriend,* we found, at least among anglophone media, that coverage of these cases was consistently in the expected postmaterialist direction. Likewise, coverage of Aboriginal issues also broadly fits the postmaterialist perspective. In the survey, journalists were asked to rank the amount of respect Aboriginal leaders should receive. Both French- and English-speaking journalists expressed a moderate view of Aboriginal leaders, which led us to expect a balanced, if not slightly supportive, coverage of Aboriginal cases. The content analysis confirmed this expectation. Eighty percent of the coverage of Aboriginal cases was factual, with the remainder twice as likely to be supportive as critical of the Aboriginal party. This finding indicates that if any portion of the study cries out for further research it is this one. Expanding the study to include prominent Aboriginal cases might provide the necessary data to test the theory in more depth.

While postmaterialist theory has economic elements, our questions on economic issues were used to find out whether journalists were supportive of capitalism. The cultural critical perspective on the media indicated that journalists might favour "responsible capitalism," but clearly expressed the view that journalists' attention to economic issues would typically support the dominant ideology of capitalism. We argued, however, that Canada cannot properly be described as a capitalist society, but that the notion of an embedded state or a politicized or "etatized" society was a more accurate descriptor. If the cultural critics were correct, we should expect journalists to oppose the status quo either by advocating genuine capitalist positions or even stronger state control. The data showed, however, that overall, journalists did not differ significantly from the public on economic questions. Both groups tend to support a middle-of-the-road position on economics, neither fully capitalistic nor statist.

However, when CBC journalists were examined separately from the private sector, a statistically significant difference did emerge. CBC journalists displayed a strong left-of-centre position on economic issues. Their position was significantly different from both the private-sector journalists and from the public. The data were confirmed by the self-placement of CBC journalists on a left-right scale, so that it seems reasonable to conclude that, compared with private-sector journalists, CBC journalists are self-consciously left wing. We noted as well that radio journalists indicated that they were more likely to say that they voted NDP than any other group, but because of the relatively small sub-sample these results were not statistically significant. However, the findings are consistent with the opinions expressed on economic issues and suggest a statist leaning for CBC journalists compared with a mixed view of private-sector journalists.

Given these views, we expected to find that CBC would provide more left-of-centre coverage on economic issues and that private media would balance left and right coverage. The major finding of our analysis of unemployment, employment, and inflation was that negative news was the most important consideration of how these economic indicators are covered. We found that the media in general over-emphasized increases in the unemployment rate while under-reporting instances when the unemployment rate went down. In the absence of negative national unemployment figures, the media typically focused on Quebec, where the unemployment rate was much higher than in the rest of the country.

In addition to the emphasis on negative news, we found that there were statistically significant differences in how the private- and public-sector journalists reported economic issues and these differences were consistent with journalists' own views on economic issues. CBC journalists' mean score for opinions on economic issues was 2.2750 out of three, where three is extremely left wing and one is extremely right wing. This indicated that CBC journalists had a moderately left-of-centre position. The combined index of causes and solutions to economic issues reported was a mean score of 2.2316, also representing a moderately left-of-centre position. All these numerical values were statistically significant.

Based on the survey of private-sector journalists we expected to find a balance of opinion on economic issues. Indeed, the private-sector journalists were placed on the centre position on economic opinions at 2.0156. The mean score for the content analysis of the *Calgary Herald,* the *Globe and Mail,* and *CTV News* was 1.9853, indicating that statistically it was significantly different from CBC and that it was nearly balanced, but balanced slightly right of centre. The conclusion we drew is that journalists neither wholly support capitalism nor are they strong advocates of state control. Coverage of economic issues typically mentioned both market and regulatory options, which provides credibility to the view that the pluralist paradigm does exist in the Canadian media.

For the francophone journalists, there were no statistically significant differences between private- and public-sector journalists on economic issues. This might have been because of the small sample size. However, the aggregate of Radio-Canada and private-sector journalists indicate that they held moderate views on the economic issues they were polled on. The content analysis also showed no statistically significant differences between private- and public-sector media, and generally speaking their coverage was balanced.

These findings provide strong evidence that the individual views of journalists do influence the way they cover the news. When journalists have left-of-centre views on the economy, such as is typical at English-speaking CBC, their reporting of economic issues is also left of centre. The more moderate views of private-sector journalists and French-speaking journalists were likewise reflected in their news coverage. Since we examined several different news organizations and found no statistically significant difference between their coverage – despite the fact that journalists themselves and others have mused that Southam, for example, was bound to reflect the strong right-wing views of the majority share-holder at the time, Conrad Black – we can conclude that journalists are indeed influential in the news that is produced with their input.

At the same time this analysis does offer some evidence that journalists support the dominant ideology. However, what we can see from our survey is that the dominant ideology within CBC at least is not capitalism, but more or less enthusiastic support for the embedded state. In contrast, the private-sector journalists were less enthusiastic "statists," but they did not typically act as cheerleaders for capitalism either.

On the question of national unity, we found that English-speaking journalists thought of themselves mainly as Canadian, whereas French-speaking journalists saw themselves mainly as Quebeckers. In this instance there were no differences in either language groups with respect to ownership. Similarly, when asked about Quebec separatist politicians, the anglophone group found them somewhat destructive, while the francophone group found them to be somewhat constructive. Similarly, on the question of partition of Quebec, the anglophone population thought that regions in Quebec should have the right to decide whether to go with Quebec or stay in Canada in the event of a "yes" vote on Quebec separation. Journalists led public opinion on this issue. On the French-speaking side, journalists were stronger in their belief that regions did not have the right to divide Quebec in the event of a "yes" vote on sovereignty.

To measure the national unity issue, we examined news coverage of partition of Quebec. Canadian politics and the media are besieged with national unity issues and one way to limit the scope of the content analysis and measure it directly with our survey was to examine partition of Quebec. In the event, partition of Quebec proved to be too narrow for our purposes, yielding only sixty-six stories for all news outlets examined for the year in question, despite the fact that it was an election year and that several prominent opinion leaders in English-speaking Canada debated the issue. Even so, the sixty-six stories yielded a sufficient number of statements, which were the units of analysis, to generate sufficient data to make statistically meaningful analyses.

As was the case in the survey, two-thirds of English-speaking media coverage presented arguments in favour of partition of Quebec. Francophone news outlets presented the "no" opinion 60 percent of the time. There were no statistically significant differences between private and public coverage in either language on this question. In other words, the coverage divided only on linguistic lines.

The data presented confirmed the view that, with respect to national unity, anglophones would uphold the dominant view that it was important to ensure the integrity of the Canadian state, whereas francophone journalists would uphold the legitimacy of Quebec nationalism. In this case, ownership had no influence; the essential variable was the language of the journalist. Anglophone journalists had very similar views to their audience, but francophone journalists were more likely to lead the public on this issue. This finding suggests that journalists do have a role as opinion leaders and the potential to influence the public by the way they cover the news. Further research should expand in these themes with respect to national unity, either by expanding the analysis to include other contentious national unity issues or by increasing the time frame of the content analysis to include more stories.

LIMITATIONS TO THE RESEARCH

The inconclusiveness of some of our results was in part a consequence of both the period we examined and the unavoidable necessity of striking a balance between relevant information and cost. French-language television coverage was the most compromised. The fact that French-language television news is not indexed or transcribed makes it difficult to obtain data. One must record and transcribe news programs, a task that is made more difficult because of time-zone differences and the intervention of sporting events and other special programs. Despite the data gaps, this study is the most thorough and quantitative analysis of Canadian media and news coverage to date.

The study was unique in that it compared public and private English and French news coverage. Moreover, journalist opinion in these groups was compared with public opinion, which also had not been done before in Canada. However, because of the decision to compare the opinions of journalists with those of the public, the journalist sample was relatively small, making it difficult to do analysis on sub-samples that would control for region or age. Additional research with larger samples might explore the differences between television, radio, newspapers, and how Internet-based news outlets compare with each other. Larger media samples would also make the results easier to generalize, especially in the case of CBC.

Journalists are a notoriously difficult group to study. We should recall that this was but one snapshot of journalists compared with news coverage. We need to know whether this snapshot produced unusual results or whether subsequent snapshots could also see links between the beliefs of journalists and their news output. We also need to measure changes within the news media in Canada to see how value orientations of journalists change and how issues develop over time. If another study were conducted with a larger journalist sample size, it would be useful to examine in greater detail the constraints journalists feel when putting the news together. This too is a difficult balancing act for the researcher because inevitably these questions require longer interview times, which in turn limit the ability of the researcher to obtain high respondent rates.

Some readers may be wondering where these findings leave us. How should journalists behave, or what can be done about these results? The short answer is that we have no firm views on how journalists should act. Even if we did, our opinions of what journalists should think or how they should behave is not the subject of this work. The point of this work is not to provide our recipe for news reporting, but rather to provide an explanatory model for why we get the news we have. Our contribution to the field it to say simply that owners do not provide the labour for the product, therefore the product does not necessarily reflect the owners' values. Instead, because journalism is in essence a human endeavour, it must reflect the values and political orientations of those who do it. To say that journalism is based on notions of objectivity is to state the ideal. What we demonstrate is that Canadian journalists have a long way to go in achieving that ideal.

When we examine the larger context of ownership and convergence we can offer some reassuring comments to those who fear this trend. Because, as we demonstrate, news stories are dependent on individual journalists writing, selecting sources, doing interviews, and so forth, the issue of who owns the company, or how large those holdings may be, does not have a large – or even small – impact. Having said that, it should be pointed out that our results do indicate that ownership matters in one respect: the hiring and firing of staff. Very clearly we found that like-minded people work in like-minded organizations. That CBC journalists had different value orientations than those in the private sector does indicate an underlying corporate culture or ideology within news organizations. Thus, the most significant thing that might happen in a change in ownership is a change in staff. Most certainly, if a new owner comes in and replaces staff with people who support his or her ideology, then clearly the coverage of the news will change.

Since we embarked on this study a number of things have changed in the Canadian media landscape. Conrad Black launched a conservative daily newspaper, the *National Post*. He subsequently sold his majority shareholdings of Southam and in time also sold the *National Post* to the CanWest Global media network, which then replaced the founding editor-in-chief, Ken Whyte. Those sales and the subsequent debate on convergence in Canada have opened up more questions about corporate ownership and journalistic freedom. They also indicate that our work is far from over. There needs to be an update of this research that reflects the changes in ownership from Conrad Black to the Asper family. We need to see if the values and ideological beliefs of journalists have changed from when we first did the study. Most important in our minds is the need to replicate our results of the correlation between journalist ideology and news content. This would not only provide necessary corroboration of our results, but also give Canadians some longitudinal data on the evolving nature of journalists in Canada. We hope to accomplish these goals in a subsequent book in the next few years.

QUESTIONNAIRE

Questions common to both genpop and journalists [no change required]

1   My name is _____ and I'm phoning for COMPAS, the public opinion research firm. You may recall receiving a letter from Conrad Winn of COMPAS saying that we would take the liberty of phoning to do a confidential interview for a university-supported research project. Could I ask you the questions now?

2   As you know, people often describe their own opinions about politics as left wing or right wing. Speaking personally, would you say your views are best described as
    ☐ Very left wing
    ☐ Left wing
    ☐ Moderately left wing
    ☐ Moderately right wing
    ☐ Right wing
    ☐ Or very right wing?

3   [Don't prompt but record a volunteered "centre" or "in the middle."] How would you describe your immediate manager of your unit or department ... Are they

☐ Very left wing
☐ Left wing
☐ Moderately left wing
☐ Moderately right wing
☐ Right wing
☐ Or very right wing?

4 [Don't prompt but record a volunteered "centre" or "in the middle."] Generally speaking, how desirable is it for Canada to have a capitalist system with free markets and individuals having the right to own property ...
☐ Extremely desirable
☐ Very desirable
☐ Somewhat desirable
☐ Not really desirable, or
☐ Not at all desirable

5 As you may know, there's been much debate about communism in the former Soviet Union. In thinking about communism, which of the following opinions is closest to your own ... [rotate]
☐ It was essentially evil and unworkable.
☐ It was at least partly evil and unworkable.
☐ It may have been a good idea, but it was wrecked by bad leadership.
☐ It was definitely a good idea but wrecked by bad leadership.
☐ It was never ever as bad as it was painted by its enemies.
☐ It was basically a good system.

6 As you know, there are some economists in universities and in research centres like the Fraser Institute who say that they believe capitalist economies, competition, and private property bring more wealth, freedom, and better health to the largest number of people in society. Would you say that there is
☐ Complete truth
☐ A lot of truth
☐ Some truth
☐ Not much truth, or
☐ No truth at all in this viewpoint?

7 Talking about wealth, a lot of people agree that changes in technology and in the global economy affect how well individuals are able to do financially. But people disagree about other factors. Some people say [rotate]

☐ that hard work, education, and personal responsibility are keys to personal success while

☐ other people say that personal success is largely determined by the power of governments and large corporations.

Which of these opinions is closer to your own?

8 Do you feel that way strongly or moderately?

9 If a provincial election were being held in your province today, which provincial party would you vote for? [Don't prompt unless respondent asks.]

☐ Conservative
☐ Liberal
☐ Reform
☐ Bloc Québécois
☐ NDP
☐ National Party
☐ None of these
☐ Other (specify)

10 For which party did you vote for in this past spring's federal election? [Don't prompt unless respondent asks.]

☐ Conservative
☐ Liberal
☐ Reform
☐ Bloc Québécois
☐ NDP
☐ National Party
☐ None of these
☐ Other (specify)
☐ Did not vote

11 At this point, I'm going to read you a list of some groups in society. On a seven-point scale, please tell me how much respect society should show to each group where seven means a lot more respect than they get today, and one, no more respect than today. First of all [rotate] ...
  ☐ Feminists or women's activists
  ☐ Environmentalists
  ☐ REAL women, the organization that favours more rights for stay-at-home mothers
  ☐ Pro-life, anti-abortion organizations
  ☐ Pro-choice organizations that favour women's rights to have abortions
  ☐ Academics who oppose too much American influence in Canada
  ☐ Aboriginal leaders
  ☐ Married couples who make every effort to be loyal and faithful to each other

12 At this point, I'm going to ask you a couple of questions about how the economy works. It is sometimes said that when Canada's economy has low inflation and prices don't change much, there is high unemployment. Do you think this statement is
  ☐ Completely true
  ☐ Largely true
  ☐ Somewhat true
  ☐ Not really true, or
  ☐ Not at all true?

13 As you know, there's been talk about the national debt. Which of the following opinions is closer to your own? [rotate]
  ☐ The problem is huge and we should make it a priority to pay it down, or
  ☐ The problem's been exaggerated by right-wing interests for their own reasons.

14 Turning now to national issues, do you see yourself mainly as a Canadian or mainly as a resident of the province you live in?

15 Thinking specifically of the separatist or sovereigntist politicians in Quebec, do you see them as
    ☐ Highly constructive
    ☐ Somewhat constructive
    ☐ Somewhat destructive
    ☐ Very destructive?

16 Do you recall hearing anything in the news about the possibility that the territory of Quebec could be partitioned or divided if Quebec became a separate country, with some land going with an independent Quebec and other land staying in Canada? [Don't prompt.]
    ☐ Yes
    ☐ No
    ☐ Do not know

17 In your view, would regions within Quebec have the right to decide whether they wish to go with Quebec or stay with Canada? [rotate]
    ☐ Yes
    ☐ No
    ☐ Do not know

18 As you know, a sensitive topic in the media today is the issue of abortion. Do you highly agree, agree, somewhat agree, somewhat disagree, or highly disagree that a woman has both a moral and legal right to decide whether to terminate her pregnancy?

19 In your view, do the rights of gays or homosexuals receive too much, somewhat much, or too little attention?

20 As you know, there's talk about whether journalists feel any subtle influence from their colleagues in their reporting. [This and the following questions to be rotated.] Let's take the CBC radio, for example. It's sometimes said that people at CBC *radio* feel that they might fit the culture of their colleagues better if they highlighted the weaknesses or hypocrisies

of business, political conservatives, or the right wing. So far as you can
tell, is this
☐ Totally true
☐ Largely true
☐ Somewhat true
☐ Not really true, or
☐ Not at all true?

How about CBC television? Would such a statement be
☐ Totally true
☐ Largely true
☐ Somewhat true
☐ Not really true, or
☐ Not at all true with respect to CBC-TV?

21 How about with respect to CBC Newsworld ...
☐ Totally true
☐ Largely true
☐ Somewhat true
☐ Not really true, or
☐ Not at all true with respect to CBC Newsworld?

22 Turning to Southam news and the Southam newspapers like the *Ottawa
Citizen*. Before Conrad Black took over ownership, it was sometimes
said that people working there felt that they could get along better with
their colleagues if they highlighted the weaknesses or hypocrisies of
business, political conservatives, or the political right. So far as you can
tell, is this
☐ Totally true
☐ Largely true
☐ Somewhat true
☐ Not really true, or
☐ Not at all true?

23 Today, at Southam, it's sometimes said that people feel they could get
along better with their colleagues and bosses if they highlighted views

that are supportive of free market or conservative political ideas. So far as you can tell, is this
- ☐ Totally true
- ☐ Largely true
- ☐ Somewhat true
- ☐ Not really true, or
- ☐ Not at all true?

24 Speaking personally, have you sensed, where you presently work, any misgivings, reservations, or criticisms about your own views or reporting on the left or right in politics? [Probe for details.]

25 Have you ever been specifically told by a boss or colleagues that your political views were inappropriate in any way? [Probe.]

26 Turning to a slightly different matter, religion, would you say that you definitely believe in God, probably do, probably don't, or definitely don't believe in God?

27 In a typical year, how often to you attend religious services apart from weddings, bar mitzvahs, or other celebrations to which you would be specifically invited?

28 Approximately how many days in a typical week would you have a beer or other alcoholic beverage?

29 Now, just a few questions for statistical purposes. Are you
- ☐ Under thirty years of age
- ☐ In your thirties
- ☐ Forties
- ☐ Fifties
- ☐ Sixty or older?

30 What's your highest level of education?
- ☐ High school or less
- ☐ Some college or university

☐ University graduate
☐ Post-graduate (e.g., MA)

31 What is your current marital status?
    ☐ Married
    ☐ Living with a partner
    ☐ Widowed
    ☐ Divorced
    ☐ Separated
    ☐ Never married

32 How many children are living in your household at the present time?

33 Do you belong to a religious denomination? ☐ Yes ☐ No [If yes, pro-
    ceed to question 34. Otherwise skip to end.]

34 Which one? [Don't prompt.]
    ☐ Roman Catholic
    ☐ Main-line Protestant
    ☐ Fundamentalist Protestant
    ☐ Jewish
    ☐ Muslim
    ☐ Hindu
    ☐ Buddhist
    ☐ Other (specify)
    ☐ No answer

Thank you

Record:
    Gender
    Language of interview
    Region

Employer
- ☐ CBC Newsworld, Radio–Canada
- ☐ CBC radio, Radio-Canada
- ☐ Provincial radio or TV networks (Radio-Québec, TVO, etc.)
- ☐ Private television (CTV, Global, TVA, etc.)
- ☐ Private radio
- ☐ Any Sun newspaper except *Vancouver Sun* and *Financial Post*
- ☐ Southam newspapers
- ☐ *Ottawa Citizen*
- ☐ *Montreal Gazette*
- ☐ *Hamilton Spectator*
- ☐ *Calgary Herald*
- ☐ *Vancouver Province*
- ☐ *Vancouver Sun*
- ☐ *Cape Breton Post*
- ☐ *Chatham Daily News*
- ☐ *Daily Star*

- ☐ *Evening Telegram*
- ☐ *Kingston Whig-Standard*
- ☐ *Kitchener-Waterloo Record*
- ☐ *Medicine Hat News*
- ☐ *Northern Daily News*
- ☐ *Observer*
- ☐ *Port Hope Evening Guide*
- ☐ *Prince George Citizen*
- ☐ *Sault Star*
- ☐ *Standard-Freeholder*
- ☐ *The Daily News*
- ☐ *The Daily Press*
- ☐ *The Edmonton Journal*
- ☐ *The Evening News*
- ☐ *The Expositor*
- ☐ *The Guardian*
- ☐ *The Nugget*
- ☐ *The Standard*
- ☐ *The Sun Times*
- ☐ *The Western Star*
- ☐ *The Windsor Star*
- ☐ *Truro Daily News*

CONTENT ANALYSIS VARIABLES

Three code sheets were developed to capture essential elements of the news stories. Each story was identified by a story number, date, news source, and placement in the newspaper or placement in the newscast. In addition, every statement was identified by a unique number and identified by the name of the source and the source's affiliation. These variables were common to all three studies. In addition, variables were constructed for each story type.

EMPLOYMENT, UNEMPLOYMENT, AND INFLATION

For unemployment, coders were asked to identify each occurrence when an economic indicator was mentioned. They were instructed to identify when the indicator was said to increase, decrease, was constant, or was simply mentioned. Additional variables captured when effects were mentioned, their causes, and whether they were solutions to problems. Each of these variables could be qualified by a positive, negative, or neutral association. For all content analysis studies a "positive" statement was one where the *speaker* made a comment that was favourable or supportive of the variable in question. For example, the statement "low unemployment is great" would be coded as a positive statement about low unemployment. Conversely, a speaker who refers to the "perniciously high unemployment rate" is making a negative statement about high unemployment. A negative statement is one in which the speaker makes a comment that is opposed to, or unfavourable to, the variable in question. Finally, a neutral statement is one in which there is no "spin" or angle on the statement in question. "Unemployment is high," for example, would be coded a neutral statement about high unemployment. The types of adjectives used to describe the indicator make it apparent how to code the statement. In addition, the association that the speaker makes with the indicator is also taken into consideration. For example, likening current unemployment rates to unemployment during the Great Depression is considered a negative statement because "Great Depression" carries a negative connotation.

Only statements in a story that relate directly to the issue are coded. A statement is defined as a single idea. Statements are broken down at commas or sentence fragments. Sometimes a reference is made to one of the issues earlier in the story or paragraph and is followed by statements arguing for or against a certain position. For example, if Pierre Fortin is criticizing the Bank of Canada for its low inflation policy and then goes on to cite three reasons why he disagrees with the policy, each reason receives one record on the database.

QUEBEC PARTITION

Three unique variables were developed for the partition of Quebec. They were "event," "aspect," and "arguments." The variable "event" describes specific incidents that lead to a discussion of the partition of Canada or of Quebec. In coding this variable, the coder attempts to answer the question "What prompted the story about partition?" or the question "In what context has this mention of partition been made?" If the statement is made during a referendum campaign or an election campaign, that campaign is the "event" within which the mention is made. If the mention is made of an election or referendum that has already been held, that campaign, even though it is in the past, is still the "event" of the mention of partition.

We considered several aspects of partition of Canada or Quebec that could be discussed in the media. Legal aspects of partition include discussions as to whether partition is permissible, or necessitated, by law. As well, any mention of the effects of legal considerations on partition or of the effects of partition on laws would be coded under the legal category of this

variable. The variable also includes values on political questions, social considerations, economic consequences, as well as consideration of Aboriginal
issues. Researchers were required to identify every statement with an event
and aspect variable.

The "arguments" category is used when media coverage refers to arguments regarding partition. There are four possible categories into which an
argument might fall: partition of Canada, for and against; partition of Quebec, for and against. The first task of the coder was to determine whether or
not any argument was being mentioned in a statement discussing partition.
If there was an argument being mentioned, the coder had to determine
under which of the four categories it fell. After this had been done, the coder
then would identify which argument was mentioned. Because some rather
complex arguments were reduced to three or four words, coders were given
a primer on each of the arguments.

SUPREME COURT DECISIONS

To capture social issues, we examined decisions of the Supreme Court of
Canada that affect public policy. To start, all Supreme Court cases for the
period we examined were catalogued by a law student. Brief summaries of
the cases that might affect our research parameters were provided to the
coders. In addition to the standard variables of date, program, etc., the Supreme Court study has three additional variables. The first identifies the
court case. The second provides details of the case. The third describes the
aspect of case discussed. Here the coders identify the main thrust of the
arguments made in the cases reported.

Details could be coded as "information," "pro," and "anti." Information is
described as a neutral, unbiased statement that favours neither of the main
parties to the case. However, if the statement either favours or is critical of
both of the parties, the statement is coded as information. A "pro" statement
describes ideas that favour or support the legal argument of the party. Generally, a party to a court case will make statements that favour his or her own
position, but so could any source. An "anti" statement is one that is critical of
the legal argument of the party being discussed. A "pro–other" comment
refers to any statement that provides an argument for or against some interest other than the two parties before the court. This "other" interest might

be an intervenor, the Supreme Court itself, some segment of society not represented by a party in court, or the government where it is not represented by a party in court.

Coders were reminded to code the statement from the viewpoint of the person who spoke. To help coders identify the correct code, we assumed that, in general, most statements by reporters are factual and should be coded as information. It was also noted that plaintiffs generally make statements that favour their own position and criticize the position of the defendants. Similarly, judges writing the majority decision typically make statements in favour of those who won the case and against the parties who lost the case.

The study also differentiated types of constitutional cases as dealing either with federalism or the Charter. Federalism cases involve disputes over the division of federal and provincial jurisdictions. Federal powers and provincial powers are listed in sections 91 and 92 of the Constitution Act, 1867, respectively. For example when the Alberta government challenged federal gun control legislation in court as an invasion of provincial jurisdiction, that was coded as a federalism case. In contrast, Charter cases involve individual applicants' claims that a government statute, regulation, or action violates their rights under the Canadian Charter of Rights and Freedoms. Rights include freedom of religion, freedom of expression, right to counsel, right to a fair trial, right to be equal before and under the law, and right to minority language education. We included law cases involving Aboriginal issues in this category. Aboriginal rights are protected under section 35 of the Constitution Act, 1982.

The "aspect" variable identifies the details that journalists consider when describing the court case. Background information about the origins of the legal dispute or about the individual parties given in the story and pre-existing circumstances external to the legal proceedings would be coded as "facts of the case." For example, the statement "Suzanne Thibaudeau was receiving $1,200 a month in child support" is coded as a "fact" statement in the "aspect" variable.

Any statement that refers to the state of legal proceedings, the legal issue to be resolved in the case, the legal arguments of the parties, the legal rulings of lower courts, or any type of legal analysis of the case that does not refer specifically to the Supreme Court's ruling in the case being discussed is labelled a "legal issue."

A reference by any source to the ruling of the Supreme Court in the case being discussed is coded as a "legal ruling." Any quotations or paraphrases of the actual ruling (i.e., reasons for decision) of the Supreme Court is also coded under this category. If a story announced that a Supreme Court ruling has been handed down, any statements describing, quoting from, or describing reaction to the ruling would be coded as a legal ruling.

"Related law" is reserved for discussion of other cases relevant to the case being discussed. This would not be a current case but an older case or one being decided in a lower court. When choosing this code, researchers were instructed to code "case" as the main case being discussed, not the older case that is being discussed for its bearing on the main case. Discussion of political support for the political positions (as opposed to the legal arguments) of the parties is coded as "political context/developments." It includes reactions and legislative initiatives of governments relating to the case at hand.

PROCEDURE

Once stories were retrieved using computerized text search engines, the coding commenced. The statement was the unit of analysis. Each statement would have an identifying number that was recorded on the paper transcripts as well as the electronic code sheet. This facilitated intercoder reliability tests, recoding, and compiling quotations. For each research topic, three tests of intercoder reliability were conducted: one in the beginning, one in the middle, and one at the end. There was an increase in the reliability score as the coding continued. Once coding was complete, researchers exchanged stories to double-check each other's coding. This ensured consistency throughout the coding procedure since coders became more proficient at making coding decisions as time wore on. Changes were updated and results were analyzed.

NOTES

Chapter 1: Why Journalists?

1 All transcripts were obtained through the National Media Archive, a division of the Fraser Institute. The National Media Archive records and transcribes the nightly newscasts of CBC and CTV. Those transcripts are available from the archive by word searches.

2 At the top of the list is the Noam Chomsky Archives, described by the site as coming "from the dean of media criticism. Some of Chomsky's best works." Other organizations promoted are the Censored Projects of the U.S. and Canada as well as the Media Watch Dog of Suppressed News. In addition, resource pages for journalists of media critics such as Mnet list predominately left-wing academics. The only Canadian media-monitoring organization that uses the pluralist perspective, the National Media Archive, was absent from those links. JournalismNet, available from <http://www.journalismnet.com>.

Chapter 2: Why the News?

1 Thus, for example, on *The National Magazine,* 3 April 1998, Peter Mansbridge introduced the guests for the "Great Canadian Trivia Quiz" in a "game show" format. Mansbridge introduced the game: "First, playing for the red team, a familiar face in Atlantic Canada, former Liberal MP for Halifax, Mary Clancy. Mary is now the Canadian Consul General to New England. So if you're ever in trouble in New England, Mary is the one to call. Tonight she's paired up with Newfoundland entertainer Kevin Blackmore. Kevin is a member of the musical comedy trio 'Buddy What's His Name and the Other Fellers,' who are currently touring a new show. Welcome to both of you. And Mary and Kevin will square off against the white team: Lynn Verge is a lawyer in Corner Brook, Newfoundland. She's the former leader of Newfoundland's Progressive Conservative Party. Lynn's partner tonight is Geoff Pevere, a *Toronto Star* columnist who is a hit with Canadian trivia fans everywhere, as co-author of the book *Mondo Canuck,* and we're glad to have all of you with us tonight."

2 We simply present the results of these studies here. A detailed discussion of the content analysis methods used follows in Chapter 5.

Chapter 3: Agents of Control or Agents of Change?

1 See LeRoy and Cooper 2000 for a case study of environmentalists, clearly an NSM, and their impact on Parks Canada.

2 Of course, one could argue that the cultural critical school of media analysis is itself a kind of postmaterialist (or soft) Marxism. We must, however, leave the exploration of the paradox of a postmaterialist dialectical materialism to another occasion.

Chapter 4: Who Staff Canada's Media?

1 Journalist results are reliable +/- 4.6 percent, nineteen times out of twenty. The general population results are reliable +/- 3.2 percent, nineteen times out of twenty. The method used to calculate these figures was the estimated sampling error for a binomial (95 percent confidence level). See Babbie 1973, 377.

2 The mean is the arithmetic average.

3 In this scale, the higher the number the more likely the respondent is "left" on capitalism and free markets. Questions 4 to 7 and question 13 were recoded into an economic conservatism index with the values of Left, Centre, and Right. The "don't know" re-sponses were recoded as missing for all variables since it is unclear how to interpret that response on the issue of economic conservatism.

Chapter 6: Economic Issues

1 Harrington (1989) as well as Robinson and Sheehan (1983) found that during election years journalists do not give bad economic news more coverage. Robinson and Sheehan argue that this is because journalists are more careful to give balanced coverage in elec-tion years.

Chapter 8: The Courts and Social Issues

1 James O'Reilly, personal interview, 4 February 1999.

Chapter 9: Findings in a Shifting Mediascape

1 See, however, the *National Post,* 7 November 2000, which ran a column by David Asper, whose family company is a major shareholder in the *NP,* along with a lead editorial taking issue with Asper's argument.

REFERENCES

Abbate, Gay. 1997. "Separatists Can Be Replaced, Black Says." *Globe and Mail,* 4 February, A1.

Abramson, Paul, and Ronald Inglehart. 1987. "Generational Replacement and the Future of Post-Materialist Values." *Journal of Politics* 49: 231-41.

–. 1995. *Value Change in Global Perspective.* Ann Arbor: University of Michigan Press.

Akyeampong, Ernest B. 1997. "A Statistical Portrait of the Trade Union Movement." *Perspectives.* Statistics Canada, Catalogue no. 75-001-XPE, 45-54.

Alberts, Sheldon, and David Steinhart. 1996. "Calgary Bucks Trend, Jobless Rate Drops." *Calgary Herald,* 12 October, A3.

Alexander, Jeffrey. 1981. "The Mass Media in Systemic, Historical and Comparative Perspective." In *Mass Media and Social Change,* ed. Elihu Katz and Tamas Szeckso. London: Sage.

Apter, David E., ed. 1958. *Ideology and Discontent.* New York: Free Press.

Atkinson, P. 1997. "Big Chains Essential to Survival of Quality Canadian Newspapers." *Canadian Speeches,* 11 May, 22-8.

Babbie, Earl. 1973. *Survey Research Methods.* Belmont: Wadsworth Publishing.

Bacchus, Lee. 1998. "'Zippergate' Turned into Media Orgy." *Calgary Herald,* 28 January, A17.

Bain, George. 1994. *Gotcha! How the Media Distort the News.* Toronto: Key Porter Books.

Banting, Keith. 1986. "Images of the Modern State: An Introduction." In *State and Society: Canada in Comparative Perspective,* research co-ordinator Keith Banting, 1-23. Toronto: University of Toronto Press.

Barlow, M., and J. Winter. 1997. *The Big Black Book: The Essential Views of Conrad and Barbara Amiel Black.* Toronto: Stoddart Publishing.

Barnow, E. 1978. *The Sponsor.* New York: Oxford University Press.

Becker, Lee, Jeffrey Furit, and Susan Caudill. 1987. *The Training and Hiring of Journalists.* Norwood: Ablex Publishers.

Bennett, W. Lance. 2003. *News: The Politics of Illusion, Fifth Edition.* New York: Longman.

Berelson, Bernard, and Paul Lazarsfeld. 1948. *The Analysis of Communication Content.* Chicago and New York: University of Chicago and Columbia University.

Berelson, Bernard, Paul. F. Lazarsfeld, and William N. McPhee. 1954. *Voting: A Study of Opinion Formation in a Presidential Campaign.* Chicago: University of Chicago Press.

Bibby, Reginald. 1987. *Fragmented Gods: The Poverty and Potential of Religion in Canada.* Toronto: Irwin Publishing.

–. 1993. *Unknown Gods: The Ongoing Story of Religion in Canada.* Toronto: Stoddart Publishing.

Black, Conrad. 1997. "Quebec Partition: The Critical Question." *Globe and Mail,* 12 February, A19.

Black, Hawley. 1967. "French and English Canadian Political Journalists: A Comparative Study." Research Report Prepared for the Royal Commission on Bilingualism and Biculturalism, September.

Blais, André, Elisabeth Gidengil, Richard Nadeau, and Neil Nevitte. 1998. "Accounting for the Vote in the 1997 Canadian Election." Paper delivered at the Canadian Political Science Association Meeting, Ottawa, June.

Blumer, H. 1970. *Movies and Conduct.* Reprint, New York: Arno and the New York Times, 1933.

Bogart, W.A. 1994. *Courts and Country: The Limits of Litigation and the Social Political Life of Canada.* Toronto: Oxford University Press.

Bohte, J., R. Flemming, and D. Wood. 1995. "The Supreme Court, the Media and Legal Change: A Reassessment of Rosenberg's *Hollow Hope.*" Paper prepared for presentation at the Annual Meeting of the American Political Science Association, Chicago, August 30-September 2.

Bryman, Alan, and Duncan Cramer. 1990. *Quantitative Data Analysis for Social Scientists.* London: Routledge.

Buechler, Steven. 1995. "New Social Movement Theories." *Sociological Quarterly* 36, 3: 441-64.

Cairns, Alan. 1988. *Constitution, Government, and Society in Canada: Selected Essays by Alan Cairns.* Ed. Douglas E. Williams. Toronto: McClelland and Stewart.

–. 1995. *Reconfigurations: Canadian Citizenship and Constitutional Change.* Ed. Douglas E. Williams. Toronto: McClelland and Stewart.

Campbell, Murray. 1992. "Quayle Steps up Attack on Television Industry." *Globe and Mail,* 21 May, A11.

Canada. 1981. Report of the Royal Commission on Newspapers. Ottawa: Supply and Services.

Canada, Senate. 1970. *Report of the Special Senate Committee on Mass Media.* Vol. 1, *The Uncertain Mirror.* Ottawa: Information Canada.

Canadian Dimension. 1996, November-December. "This publication is not owned by Conrad Black." Editorial, 4.

Canadian Press. 1997. "Manning Fanning Fears; McDonough Sees Civil War." Toronto *Sun,* 21 May, 39.

Chodak, Szymon. 1983. "Etatization, Its Concept and Varieties." *Research in Social Movements, Conflicts and Change* 5: 259-94.

Clarke, Harold D., and Nitish Dutt. 1991. "Measuring Value Change in Western Industrialized Society: The Impact of Unemployment." *American Political Science Review* 85: 905-20.

Clarke, Harold D., Nitish Dutt, and Jonathan Rapkin. 1997. "The (Mis)measurement of Value Change in Advancing Industrial Society." *Political Behavior* 19, 1: 19-39.

Clement, Wallace. 1975. *The Canadian Corporate Élite: An Analysis of Economic Power.* Ottawa: McClelland and Stewart.

Clift, Dominique. 1980. "Solidarity on a Pedestal." In *Canadian Newspapers: The Inside Story,* ed., Walter Stewart. Edmonton: Hurtig Publishers.

Clow, Michael, with Susan Machum. 1993. *Stifling Debate: Canadian Newspapers and Nuclear Power.* Halifax: Fernwood Publishing.

Compaine, B. 2000. "The Newspaper Industry." In *Who Owns the Media? Competition and Concentration in the Mass Media Industry,* ed. B. Compaine and D. Gomery. Mahwah, NJ: Erlbaum Associates.

Comstock, George. 1980. *Television in America.* Beverly Hills, CA: Sage Publications.

Cooper, Barry. 1994. *Sins of Omission: Shaping the News at CBC TV.* Toronto: University of Toronto Press.

Corcoran, Terence. 1996. "Inflation Can't Fix Unemployment." *Globe and Mail,* 15 November, B2.

Cunningham, Jim, and Carol Howes. 1997. "Alberta Jobless Rate Falls." *Calgary Herald,* 11 January, A11.

Curran, James. 1990. "The New Revisionism in Mass Communications Research: A Reappraisal." *European Journal of Communication* 5: 135-64.

Curran, James, Michael Gurevitch, and Janet Woollacott. 1982. "The Study of the Media: Theoretical Approaches." In *Culture, Media, and Society,* ed. Michael Gurevitch, Tony Bennett, James Curran, and Janet Woollacott. London and New York: Methuen.

Curran, James, Michael Gurevitch, and Janet Woollacott, eds. 1979. *Mass Communication and Society.* London: Sage Publications.

Dahlgren, Peter, and Colin Sparks. 1991. *Communication and Citizenship.* London: Routledge.

–. 1992. *Journalism and Popular Culture.* London: Sage.

Dalger, Jon K. 1996. "Voter Issues, and Elections: Are the Candidates' Messages Getting Through?" *Journal of Politics* 58, 2: 486-515.

Davis, Richard. 1994. *Decisions and Images: The Supreme Court and the Press.* New Jersey: Prentice Hall.

Delano, Anthony, and John Henningham. 1995. *The News Breed.* London: London Institute.

Delli, Carpini, Michael X, and Scott Keeter. 1991. "Stability and Change in the U.S. Publics' Knowledge of Politics." *Public Opinion Quarterly* 55: 583-612.

Demers, D. 1996. *The Menace of the Corporate Newspaper: Fact or Fiction?* Ames, IA: Iowa State University Press.

–. 1999. "Corporate Newspaper Bashing: Is It Justified?" *Newspaper Research Journal* 20: 83-97.

Dennis, Everette, E. 1997. "How 'Liberal' Are the Media, Anyway? The Continuing Conflict of Professionalism and Partisanship" *Press/Politics* 2 (Fall): 115-19.

deRoche, Constance, and John deRoche. 1991. "Racial Construction in Television Police Dramas." *Canadian Ethnic Studies* 23, 3: 69-91.

Desbarats, P. 1996. *Guide to the Canadian News Media.* Toronto: Harcourt Brace.

Dion, Jean. 1997. "Entre la partition et la redition." *Le Devoir,* 26 May, A1.

Dolik, Helen. 1998. "News Staff Back Union." *Calgary Herald,* 6 November, B4.

Driedger, Doyle S. 1996. "Black All Over: As Others Exit, One Media Mogul Bets
Heavily on Print." *Maclean's* 109 (13 May): 42-3.

Drier, Peter. 1982. "Capitalists vs the Media: An Analysis of an Ideological Mobilization
among Business Leaders." *Media, Culture and Society* 4: 111-32.

Eastland, Terry. 1997. "Partial Birth Abortions." *Media Matters,* PBS, January.

Entman, Robert M. 1989. *Democracy without Citizens: Media and the Decay of American
Politics.* New York: Oxford University Press.

Ericson, David. 1977. "Newspaper Coverage of the Supreme Court." *Journalism Quarterly*
54: 605-7.

Ericson, Richard, Patricia Baranek, and Janet Chan. 1989. *Negotiating Control: A Study* of
News Sources. Toronto: University of Toronto Press.

Evans, Peter. 1997. "The Eclipse of the State? Reflections on Stateness in an Era of
Globalization." *World Politics* 50, 1: 62-87.

Fallows, James. 1997. *Breaking the News: How the Media Undermine American Democracy.*
New York: Vintage Books.

Fishman, Mark. 1980. *Manufacturing the News.* Austin: University of Texas Press.

Fiske, John. 1992. "Popularity and the Politics of Information." In *Journalism and Popular
Culture,* eds. Peter Dahlgren and Colin Sparks. London: Sage.

Flavelle, D. 1996. "Fade to Black?" *Toronto Star,* 11 May, E1, E8.

Fletcher, F., ed. 1991. *Media and Voters in Canadian Electoral Campaigns 18.* Toronto: Dundurn
Press.

Fraser, John. 1999. "Beware the Lady Who Lunches." *National Post,* 16 June, B5.

Frizzell, Alan, Jon H. Pammett, and Anthony Westell. 1994. *The Canadian General Election
of 1993.* Ottawa: Carleton University Press.

Fukuyama, Francis. 1995. "The Primacy of Culture." *Journal of Democracy* 6, 1: 7-14.

Gagnon, Lysiane. 1981. "Journalism and Ideologies in Québec." In *The Journalists.* Vol. 2 of
Royal Commission on Newspapers, *Report,* ed. Tom Kent, 19-40. Ottawa: Ministry of
Supply and Services.

Galloway, Gloria. 1999. "CBC Sends 50 Delegates to Banff Festival." *National Post,* 18
June, A1.

Gans, Herbert. 1979. *Deciding What's News: A Study of CBS Evening News, NBC Nightly
News, Newsweek, and Time.* New York: Pantheon.

–. 1985. "Are U.S. Journalists Dangerously Liberal?" *Columbia Journalism Review:* 29-33.

Garnham, N. 1986. "The Media and the Public Sphere." In *Communicating Politics,* eds. P.
Golding, G. Murdock, and P. Schlesinger. Leicester: Leicester University Press.

Gerbner, George, Hamid Mowlana, Herbert Schiller, eds. 1996. *Invisible Crises: What
Conglomerate Control of the Media Means for America and the World.* Boulder, CO: Westview
Press.

Gibson, Gordon. 1994. *Plan B: The Future of the Rest of Canada.* Vancouver: Fraser Institute.

–. 1997. "If Quebec Goes, How Much Territory Will Go With It?" *Globe and Mail,*
4 February, A15.

Gitlin, Todd. 1980. *The Whole World Is Watching: Mass Media in the Making and Unmaking of the New Left*. Berkeley: University of California Press.

Gold, Alan. 1982. "The Legal Rights Provisions – A New Vision or Déjà Vu?" *Supreme Court Law Review* 4: 108.

Graber, Doris. 1984. *Processing the News: How People Tame the Information Tide*. New York: Longman.

Ha, Tu Thanh, and Anne McIlroy. 1996. "Tax on Child Support to End. Non-Custodial Parents Will Lose Deduction under Ottawa's Reform Package." *Globe and Mail,* 5 March, A1.

Hackett, Robert. 1991. *News and Dissent: The Press and the Politics of Peace in Canada*. New Jersey: Ablex Publishing.

Hackett, Robert A., and Yuezhi Zhao. 1998. *Sustaining Democracy? Journalism and the Politics of Objectivity*. Toronto: Garamond Press.

Hallman, E., P. Oliphant, and R. White. 1981. *The Newspaper As a Business*. Vol. 4 of Royal Commission on Newspapers, *Report*. Ottawa: Minister of Supply and Services.

Hamelin, Jean, and André Beaulieu. 1966. "Aperçu du Journalisme Québécois d'Expression Française." *Recherches Sociographiques* 8, 3: 305-48.

Handler, Joel. 1978. *Social Movements and the Legal System: A Theory of Law Reform and Social Change*. New York: Academic Press.

Harrington, David. 1989. "Economic News on Television: The Determinants of Coverage." *Public Opinion Quarterly* 53, 1: 17-40.

Henningham, John. 1995. "Political Journalists' Political and Professional Values." *Australian Journal of Political Science* 30, 2: 321-34.

–. 1996. "Australian Journalists' Professional and Ethical Values." *Journalists and Mass Communication Quarterly* 73, 1: 206-18.

–. 1998. "Ideological Differences between Australian Journalists and Their Public." *Press/Politics* 3, 1: 92-101.

Herman, Edward, and Noam Chomsky. 1988. *Manufacturing Consent*. New York: Pantheon Books.

Hetherington, Marc. 1996. "The Media's Role in Forming Voters' National Economic Evaluations in 1992." *American Journal of Political Science* 40, 2: 372-95.

Hitler, Adolf. 1939. *Mein Kampf*. New York: Houghton Mifflin.

Holbrook, Thomas, and James Garland. 1996. "*Homo Economus*? Economic Information and Economic Voting." *Political Research Quarterly* 49, 2: 351-75.

Holmes, Helen, and David Taras, eds. 1996. *Seeing Ourselves: Media Power and Policy in Canada*. 2nd ed. Toronto: Harcourt Brace.

Holsti, Ole. 1969. *Content Analysis for the Social Sciences and Humanities*. Reading, MA: Addison-Wesley.

–. 1981. "Content Analysis: An Introduction." In *Reader in Public Opinion and Mass Communication,* ed. M. Janowitz and P. Hirsch. 3rd ed. New York: Free Press.

Inglehart, Ronald. 1977. *The Silent Revolution: Changing Values and Political Styles among Western Publics*. Princeton, NJ: Princeton University Press.

–. 1990. *Culture Shift in Advanced Industrial Society*. Princeton: Princeton University Press.

–. 1992. "Changing Values in Industrial Society: The Case of North America, 1981-1990." *Politics and the Individual* 2, 2: 1-30.

–. 1997. *Modernization and Postmodernization: Cultural, Economic, and Political Change in 43 Societies.* Princeton, NJ: Princeton University Press.

Inglehart, Ronald, Neil Nevitte, and Miguel Basañez. 1996. *The North American Trajectory: Cultural, Economic, and Political Ties among the United States, Canada, and Mexico.* New York: Aldine de Gruyter.

Ip, Greg. 1996. "Catalan Contrast: Why Quebec's Economy Is Ailing." *Globe and Mail,* 26 October, D1.

Iyengar, Shanto, and Donald Kinder. 1987. *News That Matters: Television and American Opinion.* Chicago: University of Chicago Press.

Johnstone, John W.C., Edward J. Slawski, and William W. Bowman. 1976. *The News People: A Sociological Portrait of American Journalists and Their Work.* Urbana: University of Illinois Press.

Katz, Elihu, and Tamas Szeckso, eds. 1981. *Mass Media and Social Change.* London: Sage.

Kesterton, W. 1967. *A History of Journalism in Canada.* Toronto: McClelland and Stewart.

Klapper, Joseph T. 1960. *The Effects of Mass Communication.* New York: Free Press.

Knopff, Rainer, and F.L. Morton. 1992. *Charter Politics.* Scarborough, ON: Nelson.

Lang, Kurt, and Gladys Lang. 1971. "The Mass Media and Voting." In *The Process and Effects of Mass Communications,* rev. ed., ed. W. Schram and D. Roberts. Urbana: University of Illinois Press.

Lazarsfeld, Paul F., Bernard Berelson, and Hazel Gaudet. 1944. *The People's Choice.* New York: Duell, Sloan and Pears.

Lermer, George. 1984. *Probing Leviathan.* Vancouver: Fraser Institute.

LeRoy, Sylvia, and Barry Cooper. 2000. "Off Limits: How Radical Environmentalists Are Shutting Down Canada's National Parks." *Public Policy Sources* no. 45. Vancouver: Fraser Institute.

Lévesque, René. 1986. *Memoirs.* Trans. Philip Stratford. Montreal: McClelland and Stewart.

Levin, Henry. 1964. "Education and Earnings of Blacks and the Brown Decision." In *Have We Overcome? Race Relations since Brown,* ed. Michael V. Namorato. Jackson: University of Mississippi Press.

Lichter, Robert S., Linda S. Lichter, and Stanley Rothman. 1986. *The Media Élite: America's New Powerbrokers.* New York: Hastings House.

–. 1991. *Watching America: What Television Tells Us About Our Lives.* New York: Prentice-Hall Press.

Little, Bruce. 1996. "Unemployment Rate Stuck at 10%." *Globe and Mail,* 7 December, B1.

Lodge, Milton, Marco Steenbergen, and Shawn Brau. 1995. "The Responsive Voter: Campaign Information and the Dynamics of Candidate Evaluation." *American Political Science Review* 89, 2: 309-26.

Lomborg, Bjørn. 2001. *The Skeptical Environmentalist? Measuring the Real State of the World.* Cambridge: Cambridge University Press.

Lorimer, R., and M. Gasher. 2001. *Mass Communications in Canada.* 4th ed. Don Mills, ON: Oxford University Press.

McChesney, R. 1999. *Rich Media, Poor Democracy: Communications Politics in Dubious Times.* New York: New Press.

McCormack, Thelma. 1983. "The Political Culture and Press of Canada." *Canadian Journal of Political Science.* 16, 3: 451-72.

McLuhan, Marshall. 1964. *Understanding the Media.* New York: McGraw-Hill.

McQuail, Dennis. 1979. "The Influence and Effects of Mass Media." In *Mass Communication and Society,* ed. James Curran, Michael Gurevitch, and Janet Woollacott. London: Sage Publications.

Manfredi, C. 1993. *Judicial Power and the Charter: Canada and the Paradox of Liberal Constitutionalism.* Toronto: McClelland and Stewart.

March, James G., and Johan P. Olsen. 1989. *Rediscovering Institutions: The Organizational Basis of Politics.* New York: Free Press.

Marx, Karl. 1843. "Contribution to the Critique of Hegel's *Philosophy of Right*: Introduction." In *The Marx-Engels Reader.* 2nd ed., ed. Robert C. Tucker. New York: Norton, 1978.

Marx, Karl, and Frederick Engels. 1932. *The German Ideology* in *The Marx-Engels Reader.* 2nd ed., ed. Robert C. Tucker. New York: Norton: 1978.

Matas, Robert. 1997. "B.C.'s New Job Trail Work-Force Growth." *Globe and Mail,* 10 May, A8.

Mazzuca, Josephine. 2001. "Network and Local TV News Sources Remain Most Popular." *The Gallup Poll* 61, 9 (February 6).

Mendlesohn, Matthew. 1996. "Television News Frames in the 1993 Canadian Election." In *Seeing Ourselves: Media Power and Policy in Canada,* 2nd ed., ed. Helen Holmes and David Taras. Toronto: Harcourt Brace.

Meyrowitz, Joshua. 1985. *No Sense of Place: The Impact of Electronic Media on Social Behavior.* New York: Oxford University Press.

—. 1996. "Television: The Shared Arena." In *Seeing Ourselves: Media Power and Policy in Canada,* 2nd ed., ed. Helen Holmes and David Taras. Toronto: Harcourt Brace.

Miliband, Ralph. 1969. *The State of Capitalist Society.* New York: Basic Books.

Miljan, Lydia. 1989a. "Priming Canadian Media Audiences." *On Balance* 2: 6.

—. 1989b. "Network Coverage of the Environment: Objectivity or Advocacy?" *On Balance* 2: 9.

—. 1991. "The B.C. Election Campaign." *On Balance* 4: 7.

—. 1994. "Media Versus Reality: Where's the Debate in the Debate on Social Policy Reform?" *On Balance* 7: 9.

—. 2000. "The Backgrounds, Beliefs, and Reporting Practices of Canadian Journalists." Ph.D. diss., University of Calgary.

Miljan, Lydia, and Jacqueline Burns. 1995a. "Comparing Mandates: Ontario and Alberta." *On Balance* 8: 2.

—. 1995b. "The Ontario Election: How Did the Media Report the Harris Victory Compared to Rae's Five Years Ago?" *On Balance* 8: 6.

Miljan, Lydia, and Barry Cooper. 1999. "Censorship by Inadvertence? Selectivity in the Production of TV News." In *Interpreting Censorship in Canada,* ed. Klaus Peterson and Allan Hutchinson. Toronto: University of Toronto Press.

Monahan, Patrick, and Michael Bryant. 1997. "The Supreme Court of Canada's 1996 Constitutional Cases: The End of Charter Activism?" *Canada Watch* 5: 3, 4.

Morgan, Michael. 1987. "Television, Sex-Role Attitudes, and Sex-Role Behavior." *Journal of Early Adolescence* 7, 3: 269-82.

Morrison, Kate, and Lydia Miljan. 1992. "Economic Reporting: How the Networks Report the News in Good and Bad Economic Times." *On Balance* 5: 4.

Morton, F.L. 1992. *Morgentaler v. Borowski: Abortion, the Charter, and the Courts.* Toronto: McClelland and Stewart.

Morton, F.L., and Rainer Knopff. 2000. *The Charter Revolution and the Court Party.* Peterborough, ON: Broadview Press.

Mutz, Diana, C. 1995. "Effects of Horse-Race Coverage on Campaign Coffers: Strategic Contributing in Presidential Primaries." *Journal of Politics* 57, 4: 1015-42.

Nelson, Thomas, and Donald Kinder. 1996. "Issue Frames and Group Centrism in American Public Opinion." *Journal of Politics* 58, 4: 1055-78.

Nelson, Thomas, Rosalee Clawson, and Zoe Oxley. 1997. "Media Framing of a Civil Liberty Conflict and its Effect on Tolerance." *American Political Science Review* 91, 3: 567-83.

Nevitte, Neil. 1996. *The Decline of Deference.* Mississauga: Broadview Press.

Ong, Walter. 1982. *Orality and Literacy: The Technologizing of the Word.* New York: Methuen.

Pal, L. 1993. *Interest of State: The Politics of Language, Multiculturalism, and Feminism in Canada.* Montreal: McGill-Queen's University Press.

Pal, L., and F.L. Morton. 1986. "Bliss v. Attorney General of Canada: From Legal Defeat to Political Victory." *Osgoode Hall Law Journal,* 24: 141-60.

Patterson, Thomas E. 1994. *Out of Order.* New York: Vintage Books.

Patterson, Thomas E., and Wolfgang Donsbach. 1996. "News Decisions: Journalists As Partisan Actors." *Political Communication* 13: 455-68.

Pines, Burton Yale. 1994. *Out of Focus.* Washington, DC: Regency Publishing.

Popkin, Samuel. 1994. *The Reasoning Voter: Communication and Presidential Campaigns.* Chicago: University of Chicago Press.

Postman, Neil. 1995. *Amusing Ourselves to Death: Public Discourse in the Age of Show Business.* New York: Viking.

Postman, Neil, and Steve Powers. 1992. *How to Watch TV News.* New York: Penguin Books.

Putnam, Robert. 2000. *Bowling Alone: The Collapse and Revival of American Community.* New York: Simon and Schuster.

Richer, Jules. 1996. "A l'endroit des chômeurs Canadiens Ottawa aura prêché la vertu du patience." *Le Devoir,* 31 December, B3.

Riffe, Daniel, and Alan Freitag. 1997. "A Content Analysis of Content Analyses: Twenty-five Years of *Journalism Quarterly.*" *Journalism and Mass Communications Quarterly* 74, no. 3 : 515-24.

Robinson, Gertrude. 1981. "Women Journalists in Canadian Dailies: A Social and Professional Minority Profile." *McGill University Graduate Communications Program Working Paper Series,* Montreal, n.p.

Robinson, Michael J., and Margaret A. Sheehan. 1982. *Over the Wire and on TV: CBS and UPI in Campaign '80.* New York: Russell Sage Foundation.

Rosenberg, Gerald. 1991. *The Hollow Hope: Can Courts Bring About Social Change?* Chicago: University of Chicago Press.

Salutin, Rick. 1992. "After the Rodney King Verdict Rick Salutin Reassesses the Power of Pictures." *Globe and Mail,* 8 May, C1.

Saunders, J., C. Mahood, and P. Waldie. 1996. "Black Reigns." *Globe and Mail,* 1 June, B1, B3.

Sauvageau, Florian. 1981. "French-Speaking Journalists on Journalism." In *The Journalists,* ed. Tom Kent. Vol. 2 of Royal Commission on Newspapers, *Report,* 43-8. Ottawa: Ministry of Supply and Services.

Savoie, Donald J. 1999. *Governing from the Centre: The Concentration of Power in Canadian Politics.* Toronto: University of Toronto Press.

Schudson, Michael. 1989. "The Sociology of News Production." *Media, Culture and Society* 11: 263-82.

—. 1990. "Trout or Hamburger: Politics and Telemythology." *Tikkun* 6, 2: 47-51, 86.

Seguin, Rheal. 1997. "PQ Prepares to Counter Federal Role in Vote." *Globe and Mail*, 29 January, A5.

Shoemaker, Pamela, J., and Stephen D. Reese. 1991. *Mediating the Message: Theories of Influences on Mass Media Content.* New York: Longman.

Simon, James. 1996. "Media Use and Voter Turnout in a Presidential Election." *Newspaper Research Journal* 17: 38-51.

Skocpol, Theda. 1985. "Bringing the State Back In: Strategies of Analysis in Current Research." In *Bringing the State Back In,* ed. Peter Evans, Dietrich Rueschemeyer, and Theda Skocpol. Cambridge: Cambridge University Press.

Slotnick, Elliot E., and Jennifer A. Segal. 1998. *Television News and the Supreme Court.* Cambridge: Cambridge University Press.

Smith, Ted. 1988. *The Vanishing Economy: Television Coverage of Economic Affairs 1982-1987.* Washington DC: Media Institute.

Soderlund, Walter, and Kai Hildebrandt. 2001. "Does Press Ownership Affect Content? A Pre- and Post- Study of the 1996 Hollinger Corporation Acquisition of Canadian Newspapers." Paper presented at the meeting of the Association for Canadian Studies in the United States. San Antonio, TX, 14-18 November.

Solimine, Michael. 1980. "Newsmagazine Coverage of the Supreme Court." *Journalism Quarterly* 57: 661-3.

Statistics Canada. 2002. "Television Viewing Fall 2001." *The Daily*, 2 December.

Stempel, Guido, and B. Westely, eds. 1981. *Research Methods in Mass Communication.* New York: Basic Books.

Taras, David. 1990. *The Newsmakers: The Media's Influence on Canadian Politics.* Scarborough, ON: Nelson Canada.

Thorsell, William. 1996. "A Higher Inflation Rate Would Lubricate Our Stagnant Economy." *Globe and Mail,* 7 September, D6.

Tribe, L. 1985. *God Save This Honourable Court.* New York: Random House.

Tuchman, Gaye. 1978. *Making News: A Study in the Construction of Reality.* New York: Free Press.

Tunstall, Jeremy. 1971. *Journalists at Work.* Beverly Hills, CA: Sage Publications.

Weaver, David H., and G. Cleveland Wilhoit. 1986. *The American Journalist: A Portrait of US News People and Their Work.* Bloomington: Indiana University Press.

—. 1996. *The American Journalist in the 1990s.* Mahwah, NJ: Lawrence Earlbaum Associates.

Whyte, John. 1990. "On Not Standing for Notwithstanding." *Alberta Law Review* 28: 347-62.

Wilson-Smith, Anthony. 1998a. "At the TV News Peak." *Maclean's*, 2 March, 62.

—. 1998b. "Why Small Is Not Always Beautiful." *Maclean's,* 15 June.

Winter, James. 1997. *Democracy's Oxygen: How Corporations Control the News.* Montreal: Black Rose Books.

INDEX